ENLIGHTENED
REAL ESTATE

TRANSFORMING OURSELVES
AND THE WORLD AROUND US

Copyright © Barry B. Scherr, 2016

FIRST EDITION

All rights reserved.

Maharishi®, Maharishi Vastu®, Maharishi Sthapatya Veda®, Maharishi Vedic®, Maharishi University of Management®, Fortune-Creating®, Consciousness-Based Education®, and Transcendental Meditation® and other terms used in this publication are trademarks or registered trademarks used with permission or according to license.

ISBN-13: 978-0-578-17957-5
ISBN-10:   0-578-17957-1

Website: www.EnlightenedRealEstate.com
Contact: info@enlightenedrealestate.com

Sundar Publishing is a division of Sundar Corporation

Printed in the United States of America

*To my father Julius, who gave me
a love of books and ideas.
To my mother Josie, who taught me
the nature of unconditional love.*

TABLE OF CONTENTS

Introduction

Section 1 Consciousness & Real Estate

Section 2 Defining a New Paradigm

Section 3 Enlightened Real Estate

Section 4 Who, What, Where, and How

INTRODUCTION

*"It doesn't matter when you wake up,
it just matters that you do."*

Traditional Proverb

The rhythm of life is accelerating. We are living in a time of amazing discoveries – cars that drive themselves, astonishing medical advances, and technology that connects everyone instantly. We awaken each day to a world full of promise, while living in a mostly outdated built environment that does not fully support how we want to live and what we want to become.

Many communities and cities are struggling with the side effects of their success or the pain of obsolescence. Pollution, traffic, inconvenience, and high cost of living are effecting our health and longevity. We are racing ahead into a promising future, but something is getting lost – the natural flow of everyday life and the joy of being together.

For thirty years, I have been watching the built environment change and adjust to shifting priorities. Today, real estate is being shaped by even more powerful forces: the internet, the millennials' lifestyle, retirees who are still young, low interest rates, and global citizens that travel the world and see it as one reality.

Enlightened Real Estate is a close look at how we got here, and the question on everyone's mind: **Where do we go from here?**

What is ideal living? What is an ideal built environment? What makes us happy, healthy, successful, and helps us on our journey to enlightenment?

My passion has been to study how the growth of consciousness and the resulting lifestyle preferences impact the built environment. My final paper in college explored the beginning of these trends that are commonplace today. After college, I entered the commercial real estate world and enjoyed a career during a time of unprecedented expansion.

In 1988, I was invited to a series of meetings for top real estate and finance professionals, in which Maharishi Mahesh Yogi – the renowned Indian teacher who popularized Transcendental Meditation in the West – presented his ideas on the built environment. He had come to the conclusion that there was inadequate planning in existing cities and towns worldwide. I remember how startled I felt when he suggested that the built environment, the same one I was betting my future on, needed to be completely reconstructed. Now, thirty years later, we find ourselves at a junction point, due to property and infrastructure obsolescence, when there will be a massive reconfiguration of our buildings, towns, and cities.

I gradually began to understand how a world might be built that satisfies both the human outer experience of everyday life and the inner journey to higher states of consciousness. Along the way, while living in California, Florida, Switzerland, or Italy, I've had many encounters and experiences that have given me pieces of the puzzle that make up the ideas in this book.

Over time, a vision has emerged of a world that requires a different point of view with revised priorities. The realization of this new paradigm will require the collective vision of mayors, planners, developers, bankers, architects, educators, businesspeople, and citizens willing to set aside egos and conflicting interests.

Today, there is an intense desire to connect both the inner Self and the world around us. Our challenge now is to build an environment that creates a common ground for these two seemingly opposite values to come together and flourish.

Barry Scherr
Florence, Italy, Santa Monica, California,
and West Palm Beach, Florida – 2016

SECTION 1

CONSCIOUSNESS AND REAL ESTATE
The Mindset Underlying
the Built Environment

CHAPTER 1
REAL ESTATE: WHERE ARE WE NOW?

*"We shape our buildings; and afterwards
our buildings shape us."*

Winston Churchill, Statesman, 1874-1965

Today, consciousness is rising, technology is rapidly advancing, and lifestyles are evolving. Our built environment, by its inherently fixed nature, lags behind the pace of rapid changes in business, government, education, and family life. To remain competitive, buildings and communities need to reflect and support the emerging lifestyle trends that increasing consciousness brings forth.

As the twenty-first century unfolds, we face a new challenge: the velocity of modern life is creating one of the biggest threats to health and happiness in human history. **Lifestyle illnesses, created by stress and pollution, are the new plague of our time.**

We have created a society based almost purely on economics and the great engine of consumption. Since the 1940's, we have built a car-dominant culture, which has ultimately led to the unexpected consequences of traffic, pollution, and increased stress. While this model has brought an unprecedented level of affluence for many, for others it has caused the loss of community, convenience, and general well-being. There is a huge gap between the lifestyle created by the car-based culture and that which supports human happiness.

Humankind has developed increasingly advanced abilities to shape the environment. However, due to the unintended consequences of our actions, we continue to find ourselves in the midst of global crises such as climate change, wars, economic shocks, cross-border pandemics, and water shortages, many of which pose existential threats to civilization.

We need to look back at ourselves through the prism of time, to see where we have come from, and where we could go. The mindset that guides the built environment is a by-product of the expression of individual and collective consciousness over time.

Every aspect of human endeavor is in the midst of transformation. The modern ideal of the suburban 2+2+2+2 lifestyle (2 parents, 2 children, 2 pets, and 2 cars) is changing. Millennials are gravitating to a more urban, less encumbered way of life in one of the largest demographic shifts in modern history. **As our culture changes, so will the real estate we build and the wealth it generates.**

Wealth needs to be redefined as a state of blissful well-being that encompasses the full range of human experience, including financial. True success includes the ability to enjoy life, family, friends, and community, while simultaneously developing one's consciousness.

The building stock needs to be rebuilt to reflect the needs of a changing world with new priorities. The present housing inventory is not reflective of the dramatically changing lifestyle choices: smaller families, extended families living together, deferred parenthood, and a preference for convenient, urban environments. Many existing properties such as big box stores, shopping malls, and outdated office buildings need to be redeveloped.

Modern buildings and cities have been designed without taking into account all the factors that make people healthy and happy. We have underestimated the impact of the built environment on human consciousness and well-being.

Architecture and city planning should be vehicles for human evolution, not just shelter and commerce. What if every city, town, and community was redesigned to make everyone's daily routine effortless and blissful?

The built environment is a key component in developing this new paradigm. As consciousness rises, real estate will regain its central role as a positive force for stabilizing and structuring society. There are signs sprouting around the world that an enlightened approach to real estate is happening already.

This book explores the reciprocal relationship between consciousness and the built environment. **By redefining real estate as a catalyst for developing consciousness, health, and happiness, we elevate it to its full potential.** What follows is a vision of how we can reimagine and rebuild our world.

CHAPTER 2
DEVELOPING CONSCIOUSNESS

We are living in a unique moment in history. There is a great awakening taking place around the world. What does this mean? Why are we discussing this topic in a book about real estate?

Individual and collective consciousness is rising. People are waking up to the *Being* part of being human. As a result, people are starting to allocate significant time and attention to their personal evolution. This includes practices like Transcendental Meditation that develop one's consciousness in the direction of enlightenment. As people's consciousness changes, so do their desires and their interaction with the world around them.

WHAT IS CONSCIOUSNESS?

The common understanding of our experience is that we are physical creatures living in a physical world. We use our five senses to understand and interact with the environment. We use our minds to understand and analyze the world around us. Our minds depend on thinking to do this. What is thinking? What is a thought? Are they merely electrochemical reactions to outer stimuli?

If thoughts were simply electrochemical events, then where does inspiration come from? How do people have original ideas? Where do emotions and love fit in?

Thoughts are frequently modified or stimulated from outer experiences, but all thoughts come from within, from what we have identified as the mind or the Self. Some thoughts and feelings are created by physical occurrences within the body and the nervous system, but other thoughts seem to emerge by their own accord from somewhere inside of us. We all have fantasies, daydreams, and other "stream-of-consciousness" experiences.

In fact, our thinking process is made up of levels, much

like the ocean. Let's compare the most obvious, surface thoughts to a wave in the ocean. From these surface thoughts, one takes action. However, there are deeper aspects of thought that extend below the surface waves and arise from subtler and subtler levels, until the silent depths of the ocean are reached. This deepest level can be understood as the most refined level of the thinking process. Like bubbles, these very delicate thoughts rise to the surface – expanding in size as they rise – and become conscious, everyday thoughts. Thoughts emerge spontaneously and continuously in all of us. This process is simply part of who we *are*.

Just beyond the finest level of thought is the field of pure awareness. This is the source of all thought and is referred to as the field of pure consciousness, which is analogous to what modern physicists identify as the unified field. It is a state where there is no subject or object, there is merely unbounded awareness, infinite energy, and intelligence. This is the source of all human experience, thoughts, feelings, actions – everything. Similarly, physicists have discovered that subatomic particles emerge spontaneously from the vacuum state.

Every day, we interact with the outer world, have our successes and failures – our full spectrum of life's experiences – driven by these deeper, most intimate, and subtle aspects of ourselves. This is why things like meditation, yoga, art, and religion exist – to engage and enrich our lives on these profound levels.

Only by developing our inner potential, by engaging in a technique that is designed to deepen our awareness and help us utilize more of these very powerful and subtle thought processes, can we expand our personal experience of life.

We live in a time when there is a great awakening. Millions of people around the world, from every culture, religion, and political persuasion are experiencing more integration of the field of silent, inner pure conscious-

ness into their everyday, outer life. Higher consciousness brings more intelligence, love, compassion, peace, creativity, and inspiration.

It seems almost laughable to think that we were born solely to invent an app, get a mortgage, take two weeks of vacation, or watch a movie. There must be more to life than that! Our desire to help each other, our joy in being together, and our search for deeper meaning and personal evolution – these are our clues to who we really *are* and who we could *become.*

Today, humanity's collective consciousness is in the midst of a major phase transition. The transformation caused by this shift in collective consciousness is creating turbulence as people and institutions struggle to adjust. To successfully rise to the challenges now facing us, we need to awaken our inner light – the infinite field of pure, unbounded awareness that is found within each of us. As consciousness rises, everything becomes more transparent.

We need to consider how we plan to build the next phase of our buildings and infrastructure, so that this transition can shape our civilization in a positive way. It's happening anyhow, so why not use this transformation as an opportunity to create the best possible structure for an ideal society? The built environment is an essential tool for creating a stress-free, evolutionary lifestyle.

CHAPTER 3
CONSCIOUSNESS THROUGHOUT HISTORY

"The entire creation is the expression of consciousness."
Maharishi Mahesh Yogi

Consciousness is the fundamental underlying field of all human endeavor. The long, winding story of the human race is presently understood by cataloging events and locating them on a timeline. These events include culture, religion, economics, politics, wars, as well as architectural and technological breakthroughs. To truly understand history, we must recognize the changes and developments of human awareness over time.

All the events of history are like waves in the ocean of consciousness. When one pays attention solely to the individual waves, one misses the big picture, the patterns and possibilities that significantly alter the course of human experience. Deep within the vast ocean of our consciousness, beyond the surface waves of individual thought, is the infinite, reverberating field of Being, which is human awareness awake to itself. **Ultimately, human progress is driven by the evolution of individual and collective consciousness.**

THE EVOLUTION OF HUMAN CIVILIZATION

The primary purpose of human civilization has always been to provide a sustainable, nourishing, and safe environment. All societies have striven to accomplish these basic goals. The natural progression of these objectives, from basic needs to higher material and spiritual aspirations, is expressed in the following three phases of society:

1 The struggle for survival

2 Material prosperity and the rise of individuality

3 Spiritual awakening

THE STRUGGLE FOR SURVIVAL

For millennia, survival was a constant challenge for most people. Humankind mostly lived in family groups, clans, and small villages, intimately connected to the natural world. Human beings did not possess a sense of individuality as we understand it today. Each person's identity was in relationship to the family, the local environment, and their cultural belief systems. Indigenous populations around the world considered themselves communal participants in an ever-evolving world that they respected and maintained. This is expressed in various cultural artifacts: the flatness of space depicted in art, the lack of focus on the individual, the importance of cultural and religious icons, and the intimate experience of the natural world.

In modern times, the survival instinct is still prevalent despite tremendous economic and technological progress. The struggle for survival will finally end when the light of consciousness provides a foundation for a balanced and abundant society.

THE RENAISSANCE

Panorama of the historical city center of Florence, Italy

Over the course of history, there have been many notable examples of advanced civilizations that embodied transformational periods in human history: such as the ancient Egyptians, Chinese, Greeks, Romans, Mayans, and the Indus Valley culture. The advent of the Italian Renaissance represented a unique moment in civilization because, in one short span of time and in a small geographic area, it brought together advancements in the fields of philosophy, science, medicine, mathematics, architecture, art, and commerce. This rebirth of knowledge incorporated many threads of philosophical, artistic, and scientific developments from the ancient Cabalistic, Greek, Roman, and Arab thinkers. The synergy of all these influences thrust the individual to the forefront, thus creating the modern concept of man.

When the Renaissance exploded onto the world stage, it celebrated this revolutionary idea of the individual apart from the collective. **Man was redefined as an active participant in the creative forces of the universe.** The individual was free to think, discover, and explore. Art and beauty became a force to uplift the individual to the perfection of the Self and the realization of God.

One of the greatest pilgrimages of modern times is to visit those places in Italy where mankind aspired to show a universal form of beauty that transcends time and reveals the divine nature of life. This art and architecture is the embodiment of the energy and intelligence of the individual seen as a spiritual Being.

"In the Middle Ages, both sides of human consciousness – that which was turned within as that which was turned without – lay dreaming or half awake beneath a common veil. The veil was woven of faith, illusion and childish prepossession, through which the world and history were seen clad in strange hues. Man was conscious of himself only as a member of a race, people, party, family or corporation – only through some general category. In Italy this veil first melted into air… man became a spiritual individual, and recognized himself as such."

Jacob Burckhardt, Historian
The Civilization of the Renaissance in Italy

Art reflects both the consciousness of the artist and the culture in which they live. The discovery of the science of perspective during the Renaissance illustrated the transformation from a two-dimensional to three-dimensional awareness. A new sense of individuality arose, as perspective gave us a new way to measure the world. This radical shift in human consciousness resulted in artworks that depicted the world with a depth of field and an earthly realism. Perspective introduced the concept of the knower (the viewer), known (the painting), and the process of knowing (viewing) as a mathematical reality expressed on a flat plane.

This rise of individuality was accelerated by impressive advances in nutrition, medicine, and commerce. The organization and culture of the Renaissance city-state created a more secure lifestyle that allowed for sufficient time and energy for the creative, analytical, and scientific thinking necessary to advance civilization.

The development of new navigational techniques and advanced shipbuilding technologies led to the rise of bold exploratory missions. Christopher Columbus discovered the New World, and Magellan circumnavigated the Earth. Through Copernicus' and Galileo's radical scientific breakthroughs, people realized that the entire universe did not revolve around the Earth, but rather the Earth revolved around the Sun. These disruptive discoveries led to an entirely new way of seeing the world and served as a catalyst for the development of the modern age.

THE MODERN AGE

"Through the window of science, we see the dawn of the Age of Enlightenment."

Maharishi Mahesh Yogi

Once again, there is realization that a massive transformation is happening in the world – a new Golden Age. This is the rediscovery of the value of the inner aspect of life. The concept of personal fulfillment solely through the outer, material world has expanded to encompass the inner exploration of consciousness. There are three phases of the modern era that signal a great awakening of consciousness.

1950's – 1970's: The Political Age
Politicians and political activity were the predominant driving factors. There was the beginning of a spiritual awakening and cultural change during this time, which became dormant with the emergence of the Economic Age.

1980's – 2010: The Economic Age
Economic factors became the main driving force in society, but the abrupt financial crisis of 2008 demonstrated the limitations of the economic model to provide a stable and meaningful life for everyone.

2010 – Present: The Beginnings of a Golden Age

Spiritual and quality-of-life issues become the predominant driving focus. Rising collective consciousness is the catalyst for a major transformation of society and the built environment.

For the first time in human history, the basic necessities of healthcare, housing, and food are being obtained by an increasing percentage of the world's population. The success of the Economic Age has allowed more people the time and energy to focus on their spiritual growth. These developments represent a historical shift in the destiny of mankind. This rising consciousness is quietly transforming business, art, science, civic endeavors, and the built environment. We are leaping forward into a dynamic, multidimensional concept of the world spurred on by the discovery of relativity, quantum mechanics, and subsequent breakthroughs in astrophysics, medical, and computer technologies.

Contemporary California represents the culmination of powerful forces unleashed five hundred years ago in Florence, Italy. A set of circumstances, similar to those which formed the Renaissance, came together in California in the mid-twentieth century; the spiritual and social revolutions of the 60's, the clustering of great universities, the influx of talent, brainpower, and sufficient wealth to create the phenomena of Hollywood and Silicon Valley. This entrepreneurial, creative culture in California created a marketplace of ideas instead of objects.

This startling burst of Californian creativity has connected everyone through technological and cultural innovation. In 2007, the arrival of the smartphone changed the world. When Steve Jobs unveiled the first iPhone, few people understood how much of a game-changer this little device would become. By 2015, approximately fifty percent of the global population used a smartphone. By 2020, this number will be almost eighty percent. This is an unprecedented development that fulfills one of the greatest aspirations of mankind - the interconnectivity of everyone.

As this dramatic explosion of technology has swept the globe, there has been a simultaneous and correspondingly impressive surge of interest in the journey inward to experience the higher Self. The rising enthusiasm for yoga, meditation, healthy food, and global exploration confirms this trend. As world consciousness becomes more refined, people will seek opportunities for stress relief and maximizing their health and happiness.

The challenge before us is to integrate the inner and outer values of life, where everyone is naturally living two hundred percent of life: one hundred percent inner, spiritual joy, along with one hundred percent outer, material satisfaction. **This is the true birthright and destiny of every human being.**

The ruins of past civilizations remind us of the ways of life and the states of consciousness of individuals who have lived in various moments in time. Real estate is the most vivid, lasting, and interactive reminder of what has come before. As consciousness rises, the purpose of the built environment evolves from providing shelter and comfort to the creation of structures that allow one to experience the unseen field of consciousness.

CHAPTER 4
THE IMPACT OF THE ENVIRONMENT
ON DAILY LIFE AND CONSCIOUSNESS

*T*he quality of our consciousness is determined by the state of our physiology. We experience our physiology through our mental clarity, emotions, overall health, and a general sense of well-being. The highest goal of society should be the creation of environments that, by their structure and amenities, allow for a healthy, satisfying, and evolutionary way of life. The environment and our physiology form a multifaceted relationship that includes physical, emotional, intellectual, and spiritual dimensions.

People lived in villages for much of human history. For millennia, the range of human activity was limited by how far a person could walk in one day. We have changed our environment, but <u>we</u> haven't changed. We continue to tie our sense of place to our immediate surroundings, our neighborhood. Over time, our physiology and psychology become intimately intertwined with the local culture and *Laws of Nature*. This passionate attachment to, and interdependency with, one's local environment is a basic human quality that has been diluted by the stresses and demands of modern life.

The Industrial Revolution, and the subsequent arrival of the automobile, propelled humanity out of this ancient pattern of small, intimate communities. Time and work were standardized. With the advent of electricity, the Sun was no longer the primary source of illumination and heat for the first time in human history. All these factors removed people from the ancient relationship between the natural environment and daily life.

The real world is a flowing, connective ecosystem. Humans once had an intimate and interdependent relationship with the environment. It is through an increasingly out-of-date mindset that our environment is seen as somehow separate from us. We're not lacking the ability to understand this situation, it's just that we've grown desensitized to our natural surroundings.

When we reestablish our intimacy with the environment, we spontaneously reach a new level of happiness, health, and prosperity. Natural spaces with pure air, water, and food are not luxuries, but the basic elements for a healthy life. In Asia, they have a special word for "forest bathing"– Shinrin-yoku (森林浴) in Japanese and Sanlimyok (산림욕) in Korean – which describes a leisurely visit to a forest in order to reduce stress and reconnect with nature and one's higher Self.

Our understanding of the environment should include the notion of a seamless connection between the natural and built environments. By siting buildings with respect to the geographic and climatic conditions, and by utilizing natural building materials that last for generations, we create a basis for humans and nature to coexist peacefully.

The principle intention of any real estate endeavor should be to create a sustainable system that brings people together and supports their personal evolution. The environment influences the structure of our daily routine. Everything we do is either facilitated or limited by the choices around us.

The primary resources of each family are time, energy, and wealth. These elements are augmented or depleted by the quality of the built environment. **Developing a lifestyle, in which our surroundings actually improve our existence, should be the goal of _Enlightened Real Estate_.**

The concept of an Ideal Village[1] represents the next stage of history of the man-made environment. It reconciles the natural environment, the built environment, and the

---

[1]The Ideal Village concept is the building block of an _Enlightened Real Estate_ community. It's a holistic, revolutionary approach to village design that is outlined in detail in Section 3.

human desire for the expansion of life and prosperity. What if every place could be beautiful, peaceful, environmentally sustainable, and abundant?

CHAPTER 5
THE EVOLUTION OF THE CITY

The village of Merano (pictured above) is the capital of the Alpine region of South Tyrol in Northern Italy. It is a unique environment of clean air, water, and food, where the level of social problems is extremely low. As a result, the government is able to use its resources for the improvement of society. A coherent environment with a high quality of life and rich community eliminates many societal challenges.

As we evolve, so do the places where we live. We create new spaces to reflect our vision of life and our priorities. **The future of humanity is becoming increasingly interdependent with the future of urban environments.** Imagine cities designed with a new goal in mind – health, happiness, and enlightenment for its citizens.

The structure and planning of Renaissance city-states offer clues for solving many of the challenges facing today's urban areas. These historical city centers in Europe offer a wonderful quality of life and have been the most admired tourist destinations for centuries. These original human scale cities, built of ancient stones, remind us of a time before cars, when people had a strong sense of community and local identity.

They show us remnants of the way we lived and interacted for millennia. Furthermore, the proliferation of timeless, beautiful art and architecture uplift those who live and visit there. We see how cities can be built to accommodate commerce, convenience, spontaneous socialization, and the celebration of human creativity.

The rise of the city-state was created by a unique combination of technological breakthroughs and a creative, ambitious merchant class. Renaissance bankers and merchants began to take responsibility for society, exhibiting qualities of intelligence and farsightedness that came from the affluence and the heightened consciousness of the time. The Italian Renaissance city-state model remains a template for the way we could structure our present-day, urban world.

History repeats itself. In the past one hundred years, New York City has become a virtual city-state, much like Venice was at its zenith. It is fascinating that New York and Venice inhabit almost the identical latitude and that each features a large natural harbor with many islands. At its height, Venice was at the confluence of advanced shipbuilding, modern commerce, and political sophistication. The Venetians' far flung trading expeditions to Africa, Asia, and Europe resulted in the importation of many new ideas, philosophies, and technologies.

Over time, the wildly diverse societies of the world have grown into greater and greater interdependence, giving rise to the phenomena of globalization and massive cross-pollination of ideas. Despite the problems brought on by globalization, this remarkable development has brought the world's populace together in ways hardly imaginable even ten years ago.

World culture is presently experiencing another major shift, even more profound than those experienced during and after the Renaissance. A tsunami of urbanization is occurring worldwide. It's a change in the way we choose to live. People are coming to the cities for personal achieve-ment, community involvement, and the excitement and energy of new cultures and opportunities. The growth of major cities from around the world – New York, Los Angeles, London, Singapore, Shanghai, Dubai, Lagos, Tokyo, New Delhi, Milan, Moscow, and São Paulo – illustrate the rise of these globally-interconnected, modern city-states.

A city is a living, breathing collection of people who both individually and collectively evolve, influenced by their surroundings, daily routine, and fellow citizens. The pro-cess of personal evolution causes lifestyle changes that reverberate throughout the architecture, communities, business, transportation, and priorities of city life. Con-verging with this globalized urbanization is the emergence of a higher goal for humankind – enlightenment.

Consciousness, the built environment, along with geo-graphical and climatic conditions have always interacted. The difference is that today we have the energy, technology, wealth, and creativity to alter buildings and cities to suit our needs. As the spiritual evolution of the individual becomes the goal of city life, future development will reflect that change in the way cities are constructed.

THE NEW GLOBAL CITIZEN

*"I feel loyalty and love for my country,
but I also feel something for my world."*

Julius Scherr, Author's Father, 1914-2004

This time of transformation has created a new lifestyle and identity for people: the new global citizen. The current widespread diffusion of ideas and infrastructure has gen-erated a new way of life, particularly in major metropolitan areas. These major cities, with their focus on economics, high culture, and luxury, have created a lifestyle to which millions of people around the world aspire. Global citizens freely migrate between these vibrant urban centers and feel comfortable anywhere. The advent of this lifestyle has set off a competition among international developers to design the most sophisticated living spaces imaginable.

Still, the real question remains: why are people running from city to city? The obvious answer is found in the variety of cultures they discover, and the opportunities and experiences they cultivate. Everywhere they go, they are searching through the avenues of life to find happiness and success.

The rise of natural havens such as Aspen, Cape Cod, Mallorca, Costa Rica, St. Barts, Jackson Hole, Sun Valley, Lake Como, and Costa del Sol are an antidote to life in the big city. This is a metaphor for the inner and outer value of life – people are moving around to try and find happiness, as none of these environments are making them feel one hundred percent comfortable. City life is too frenetic, while country life is too quiet.

Up to one hundred years ago, there was a tribal sense of roots, as most people lived their whole lives in the same village or town. Remnants of this idea are still prevalent today, as you will hear many Italians say they are Florentine, Roman, Sicilian, or Venetian, before Italian. People used to identify themselves with a place; now they are looking to establish themselves in the place that most suits their personal and professional goals. As the chaotic modern world has uprooted many of these global citizens, they are looking to reestablish balance and a sense of belonging.

This goes to the heart of the matter: we need to be rooted in ourselves, as well as create an environment that is so charming that we don't want to leave. The new global citizenry is looking for wholeness of experience – an environment that satisfies their desire for the best the world has to offer, as well as a culture that encourages personal evolution.

Cities will evolve to meet the needs of the new global citizens by combining modern technology with a more natural, conscious way of living. Today, these new global citizens are demanding greater opportunities, better amenities, and a more balanced lifestyle, which signals emerging interest in a life based on higher goals. As interest grows in many spiritual and natural ways of life, we are starting to see new real estate asset classes emerge. We need a modern version of a classic Renaissance city-state that can transport us effortlessly into an Age of Enlightenment.

"Built architecture is always a mirror of 'the state of civilization' of a particular place and time, irrespective of the nature of the building and its financial underpinning."

Extract from the Foreword by Christoph Thun-Honenstein
in Uneven Growth: Tactical Urbanisms for Expanding Megacities
by Pedro Gadanho

CHAPTER 6
THE ILLUSION OF SEPARATENESS

"Things don't matter, people do."

Josephine Scherr, Author's Mother, 1917-2010

Following the Depression and World War II, Americans were emotionally drained, as well as physically and spiritually fatigued. All they wanted was a little patch of suburban heaven. Since then, our culture has gradually become adapted to what might be called the "Illusion of Separateness." This is the misconception that each of us is somehow emotionally independent from others, and that we live in a personal bubble of privacy made possible by sufficient affluence. This contrivance is just that – a creation of convenience that has turned very inconvenient.

We have adopted this culture of personal privacy to try to keep the world at bay, to be protected from the uncertainty, and the sometimes chaotic, stressful nature of modern life. In America, this sense of separateness began to arise when the suburban, impersonal, car-based lifestyle became commonplace. The unprecedented rise of a vast middle class since the 1950's has brought with it the notion of privacy as a marker of a successful life. Since then, our society has gradually been sliding into an emotionally disconnected mode of existence, with the resulting loss of community. At stake is one of the most fundamental life experiences that makes us happy: sharing our life with others. The truth is that we are utterly dependent on one another in a myriad of ways.

The idea of a joyful, suburban existence devolved into an isolated, inconvenient lifestyle. This phenomenon has especially affected our young people. At the very moment in their lives when they most need socialization and community, they have become withdrawn. Video games, social media, and computers are not a substitute for friendship and outdoor activities.

It's no coincidence that many of the most popular movies and TV shows like Friends, Seinfeld, and Modern Family are built around the family and friendship experience. People are hungry for a less complex, more emotionally-connected world.

Dr. Stewart Wolf, author of *The Power of Clan*, said "People are nourished by other people." He went on to say that the characteristics of tight-knit communities are better predictors of healthy hearts than low levels of serum cholesterol or tobacco use.

In the 1950's and 60's, there was a very revealing scientific study by Dr. Wolf and John Bruhn that discovered "The Roseto Effect." Starting in the 1930's, a large number of Italian immigrants moved to Roseto, a small town in Pennsylvania. They discovered that the incidence of mortality due to heart disease dramatically increased when they started adopting a more suburban American lifestyle. To the researcher's surprise, the data indicated that the increase in heart disease was due to the second generation's loss of a sense of place, community, and traditions, rather than a casualty of the American diet.

Just as the nutritional content in food is necessary to create a healthy lifestyle, a nutritious emotional life is equally necessary for the nourishment of body and soul. The people of Roseto brought more than just their luggage to America, they also brought their tradition of togetherness – their overflowing dinner tables, church parades, after-dinner walks, and social clubs for every interest – which contributed to their health and well-being. In essence, they nourished their minds, bodies, and spirits as an act of daily celebration.

A tremendous amount of money has been spent on research to combat heart disease. Poor diet, lack of exercise, and stress have all been identified as causes of this epidemic. However, a lack of community-based living has created isolation and loneliness, which has emerged as a significant risk factor. An inefficient, car-centric lifestyle creates dis-connection.

With the widespread overemphasis on work and career, it is no surprise that heart disease has become the leading cause of death. Modern life is characterized by people identifying themselves by what they *do*, rather than who they *are*. It is time to reevaluate how to reverse this cultural separation.

Stress and isolation leads to cascading personal and social problems. If anxiety and loneliness are allowed to build up, people begin to lose faith in themselves and each other.

> *"Some forms of chronic stress don't involve argument or debate, but they are just as damaging. High on the list is loneliness... Lonely people are more apt to have high blood pressure, fragmented sleep, and diminished immunity."*
>
> Nathan Seppa
> "The Mess That Is Stress," Science News

As the twenty-first century unfolds, we are gradually seeing the full implications of what a disconnected world looks like. This disconnection needs to be dealt with at the source by having people live in a more ideal, connected environment. One of the great joys of life is being together, enjoying family, creating communities, and having enduring, life-sustaining relationships.

This needs to be reflected in the way our communities are built. Even a large city can have an identity that allows each family to be part of their neighborhood and the city as a whole. We're now reawakening to the enjoyment of village communities within a city, like the Quartiere of Italian cities or the various villages in New York – such as Greenwich Village, the East Village, Williamsburg, etc. As cities develop, city planners should consciously curate neighborhoods to support and inspire their residents, while encouraging spontaneous connection.

The built environment needs to create spaces for emotions to flow effortlessly and joyfully. The illusion of separateness is just that – an illusion. If planned and executed correctly, we can create spaces and neighborhoods that are uplifting, interactive, safe, and beautiful, all contributing to the highest goal of an ideal society.

CHAPTER 7
THE HUMAN ENERGY CRISIS

*I*n recent years, the world has experienced a massive expansion of the western, consumption-based lifestyle. Capitalism has helped many millions of people rise out of extreme poverty. Useful, game-changing technologies are leap-frogging across the globe.

Economic systems exist to provide opportunity and unleash maximum human creativity and progress. However, these systems should encourage every aspect of life to flourish in the light of health, happiness, joy, financial success, and environmental responsibility.

The overemphasis on activity to the point of exhaustion is creating a society which struggles to solve basic problems and reflects an incomplete understanding of the human experience. We are the masters of our destiny, and we must intentionally create with both hands – not create with one and destroy with the other. The world that sent a man to the moon, that cured almost every major disease, and that can fathom the mysteries of the cosmos can certainly learn to create without negative side effects.

We have become addicted to the speed and intensity of modern life. This tends to erode one's state of well-being, often to the point of creating an inability to rest, enjoy, and grow. One can easily get caught up in busyness and lose the natural connection to one's inner compass, and thus to nature itself. We all experience the fatigue created by too much time spent driving, working, and maintaining the household. Phrases like, "work hard, play hard" and "I can rest when I'm dead" are commonplace. The boundaries between work and life have been blurred, which allow for flexibility, but also encourage a lack of downtime. Technology-driven activities, such as social media, minimize time spent engaging in face-to-face interactions. **How did we end up with such an exhausting daily routine where we rush through everything?**

The endless, exhausting race against time is compounded by:

1 Tiredness due to overworking

2 Lack of progress due to short-term thinking

3 The inconvenience and poor planning of the built environment that creates traffic jams, long commutes, dispersed amenities, and an impersonal society that is difficult to navigate

Economic cycles are partially caused by individual and collective burnout through overwork and stress. If it's all about being the best, working the hardest, and burning the midnight oil, then why haven't we solved all the world's problems yet? The overemphasis on work creates chronic fatigue and is detrimental to family life, personal health, and spiritual development. Such confused priorities need to be balanced by a daily routine that maintains a rested physiology. Bigger, cheaper, and faster are not necessarily a recipe for happiness and long-term economic prosperity.

The real energy crisis is one of human energy. Rest is the basis of effective activity. A tired person sees the world through the lens of limitation. A rested person sees problems as an opportunity for change and transformation. Imagine a society where people are fresh, ready, and alert – more able to meet the challenges of a complex world. There is a growing awareness that a balanced physiology is required to live a joyous, fulfilling life.

The built environments of the future will have to facilitate the ease and flow of the day and help mitigate the crisis of debilitating stress. If we think about human energy as a flow, it can either be blocked by too much exhaustion and aggravation or flow smoothly and allow for people to enjoy their day-to-day existence. Once these hurdles have been removed, then there is time for connection and ultimately spiritual growth.

We are becoming more aware that the condition of the human physiology drives experience; it creates the way

we feel and how we experience the world. This represents a fundamental shift in perspective, an awakening to the true possibilities of our human potential. **There is a higher purpose for the human physiology: the expansion of consciousness.**

CHAPTER 8
THE NEXT GENERATION LIFESTYLE

"Millennials want something authentic and real.
They are more into experiences than things."

Jill Black, Philanthropist

*I*f you're feeling worried about the future of humankind, just spend some time with the millennials. Millennials were born from 1980 through the late 90's and comprise an even larger group than the Baby Boomers. They're not interested in the same things as previous generations. Millennials prefer to network, travel, and experience different cultures, rather than overindulging in the mindless acquisition of things. As citizens of a technologically-connected world, these young people are unintentionally ushering in a modern culture that demands greater environmental sensitivity and heightened community connections.

The dream of the post-World War II generation was the suburban lifestyle. The millennials see that lifestyle as lonely and isolated. The Baby Boomers, who were born into a time of the hyper-expansion of material possibilities, are joining the millennials in demanding an environment that doesn't require endless compromise. Born of different experiences, they have come to a similar conclusion: life is to be enjoyed and savored.

Their next generation lifestyle includes dramatic changes to the status quo. Millennials often live in groups; they are less concerned about privacy. They prefer smaller dwellings and to be in the middle of things, with access to all the amenities one might need for an easy daily routine and more cultural stimulation. They are dedicated to life lived with clean air and water, healthy food, public transport, and mixed-use, walking environments. Many are seekers of enlightenment, evidenced by the explosive popularity of techniques for self-realization such as yoga, meditation, juice fasts, and spiritual retreats.

Behind all these lifestyle changes is a desire to share life again – the reawakening of one of our most rewarding and fundamental impulses. This comes from higher consciousness and will transform the real estate landscape at an astonishing speed.

The millennial reality includes a clear awareness of the future, along with the strong desire to live life in the moment. The millennials are, in some sense, living their own version of the 1960's. They represent a similar cultural awakening, while facing much less resistance from the established order. They are displaying qualities of field independence – the ability to see through what's around themselves and to think and live originally. With a little guidance from everyone else, they will fix the mess that out-of-touch special interest groups are promoting, simply because they won't patronize these intermediaries who are orchestrating an unhealthy world.

In the workplace and as entrepreneurs, they are often fearless and passionate about making the world better through their businesses, thus narrowing the gap between work for individual gain and societal harmony. Many feel they are on a mission. They've learned that it's okay to fail and try again. They use technology to create and market businesses faster than ever. They have seen the ebbs and flows of employment and business, and they want to control their own destiny.

Millennials are making a unique contribution to the evolution of human civilization. They are the first generation en masse to make the connection between consciousness and daily life. The quest for enlightenment was always considered a private concern, practiced alone or in an ashram. The idea that yoga, meditation, and a healthy diet would be a priority of one's daily routine, while also being active in the world, was a concept lost in time.

Now, as they prepare to marry and have children, they're taking an integrated approach towards how they consciously design their lives and where to live. Many millennials recognize that there are four important values in life: family and friends, community, prosperity, and moksha (enlightenment). They will turn every concept of real estate that relies on the old, impersonal, and separate model upside down.

Enlightened Real Estate enlivens the silent, invisible quality of the built environment to satisfy the desire of the next generation to connect with their higher Selves. The millennial generation sees life as a kaleidoscope of experience created by both individual and group efforts. Simultaneously, real estate is waking up from the long sleep of pure functionality into a time when inspiration, beauty, and community will dominate. The man-made environment can give us an experience that enlivens every particle of our Being, while offering safety and security, and creating space for variety, diversity, serendipity, fun, and adventure. The era of look-alike malls, strip centers, offices buildings, and housing tracts that helped send half a generation into boredom, and even depression, will be replaced by a thousand Ideal Villages in every size and format that will provide the stage for a Golden Age of real estate.

A major breakthrough is coming from the insights, discoveries, and preferences of the millennial generation. The future of real estate is interactive and full of potential to transform daily life and human consciousness. It can be focused on the synergy and convenience that comes from a truly mixed-use, walking village, in which a variety of human activities are taking place simultaneously, replacing the narrowly defined asset classes of the past – retail, office, industrial, educational, and residential.

Millennials are looking to the real estate world for solutions. They want positive experiences – that's what they will buy or rent – therefore developers and property owners need to think of themselves as lifestyle curators, instead of builders, managers, and salespeople of square footage. This isn't just easy access to a pool or gym, but a lifestyle of togetherness, sharing, belonging, and ultimately evolution.

41

Successful developers will study the design and function of the antique European city centers, just as Palladio measured the Roman ruins to find out the secrets of perfect proportion. Ideal Villages will spring up, filled with vastu[1] buildings and all sorts of wonderful energy saving and producing technology. The next phase of economic expansion will be in infrastructure and buildings for health, happiness, and spiritual growth!

The millennials think differently because they are different. They are focused on creating a lifestyle that cultures a holistic, fulfilling reality. *Enlightened Real Estate* meets the demands of the millennial generation. Their Villages will be lighthouses of possibility, and their generation will be remembered as a pivotal point in the story of humankind.

> *Young people today tend to view others through the lens of acceptance, rather than judgment, favoring connection over separateness.*
>
> Mary Waldon, MSW, LCSW

---

[1] The science of vastu architecture is the most ancient and complete system of architecture and planning. Focusing on the underlying proportion, placement, and orientation of communities and buildings, the principals of vastu are universal and can be applied to any architectural design style worldwide. At its core, vastu architecture connects individual life to the holistic value of nature's intelligence. Maharishi Mahesh Yogi's restoration of the knowledge and practicality of vastu for the modern world is referred to as Maharishi Vastu or vastu throughout the book. Further details about vastu are included in Chapters 18 and 23.

SECTION 2

DEFINING A NEW PARADIGM

CHAPTER 9
RISING CONSCIOUSNESS AWAKENS GENIUS

*"Genius is not that you are smarter than everyone else.
It is that you are ready to receive the inspiration."*

Albert Einstein, Physicist, 1879-1955

A global rise of consciousness is now sweeping our planet. The velocity of change in every aspect of life threatens institutions and ideas that have stood for generations. The wave of transformation is unstoppable, inevitably flowing in one direction: toward a future of greater awareness.

The disorientation that many are feeling is a reaction to the worldwide increase of consciousness. The granular, zoomed-in view reveals stubborn pockets of ignorance, fear, and resistance. The zoomed-out perspective is one of phenomenal growth of consciousness and the rise of the global citizen.

While enlightenment was once seen as an ancient spiritual goal for the monastic few, today it is no longer considered a far-fetched idea, but rather a state of consciousness attainable by anyone. **Enlightenment is a state where one has fully integrated inner silence into everyday life, resulting in twenty-four-hour bliss, and full support from the environment to manifest one's desires.** The widespread interest in enlightenment we see today is a sign of the dawning of a new time for mankind.

An enlightened physiology can express genius. The geniuses of the Renaissance honored at the Uffizi Gallery in Florence altered the course of western civilization in ways that still inspire us today. It is a wonderful reminder of why the Renaissance was called the "Age of Genius." We are entering into another renaissance fueled by technological advancement, globalization, and expanding human potential.

We rarely discuss the origin of genius. What is the secret sauce that somehow drives the creative energy of an individual? How can genius be increased despite the stress of modern life?

Is it genetic?

Is it talent?

Is it education?

Is it wealth?

Is it social connections?

Is it having a purpose?

Is it determination?

Is it luck?

Is it a positive attitude?

Is it doing something you love?

While genius may be associated with many of these attributes and influences, its basis lies far beyond the reach of the everyday intellect. Genius is the experience and understanding of consciousness as the prime mover of life. It is the quality through which great talent, creativity, and persistence transforms the way we see, experience, and live in our world. Individual genius develops from the unseen field of consciousness and becomes visible through ideas, inventions, artwork, or buildings.

Ingenious inventions and insights transform everyday life on a profound level. If Einstein hadn't come along, how many years would it have taken us to discover relativity? What about Steve Jobs' iPhone or Elon Musk's Tesla? As geniuses tap into the unified field, they apply the intelligence of nature to scientific theory to improve everyday life through innovation.

As we wake up the blissful field of pure consciousness inside ourselves, we experience the field where all knowledge and solutions reside. Film director David Lynch calls it *"Catching the Big Fish,"* the next great idea that can be cultured to become a great accomplishment in life.

The rate of change in the last fifty years has accelerated the speed at which the world adopts new ideas and inventions. The compass took fifty years to gain traction on a worldwide scale; the smartphone took less than ten years.

The faster adaptation of game-changing technology is an expression of rising consciousness and interconnectivity worldwide.

Throughout history, there have always been examples of genius. With the present day phenomena of rising consciousness, genius, like wealth, will be a more common facet of everyday life. Our world, now more than ever, desperately needs lots of people exhibiting the gift of genius: more creativity, greater intuition, and a direct connection to the infinite intelligence of nature.

Progress depends on genius to connect the dots. Like a climber on the mountain top who sees the whole valley, a genius often sees beyond the horizon. Geniuses frequently create marvelous things that we didn't even know we wanted. It is this quality that brings a fascinating aspect to genius – the surprise value that opens our mind to greater possibilities, seeing beyond the current paradigm and conventional logic. In some cases, it is unbelievable persistence, which causes nature to reveal its secrets. As we discover the mysteries of the cosmos, we uncover the *Laws of Nature*. When these *Laws of Nature* are revealed, innovation abounds.

Creativity, vision, and genius are critical in advancing the structure of society. Today, the biggest challenge for real estate development is to start building for the future, instead of mindlessly replicating outdated asset classes. We have clues from historical city centers and the principles of vastu architecture to guide us to build ingenious, life-enriching *Enlightened Real Estate*. Higher consciousness will allow us to see through the limitations of our legal and regulatory environment, past the crippling planning codes, and beyond the limited risk profiles of financial institutions. As a result, a new vision of a world where being together in extended family or friend compounds, walking to work and school, more efficient transportation, and clean air, energy, water, and food will become the norm.

We are beginning to rediscover how profoundly the

environment influences the state of our physiology and even the creation of genius. We can further culture ingenuity through a healthy, happy, and consistent daily routine that is unburdened by the stress of modern life. Each human has the touch of genius; it just needs to be awakened.

CHAPTER 10
THE FIELD EFFECT OF CONSCIOUSNESS

"The term 'Laws of Nature' refers to all the laws of Physics, Biology, Chemistry, etc., including the laws that structure life at the individual and social levels, and which maintain order in the infinite diversity of the universe."

Dr. Tony Nader, M.D. - Ph.D.
Human Physiology - Expression of Veda and the Vedic Literature

We live in a time when invisible fields have more and more influence over our way of life. Starting with radio and television, and then cell phone and wireless waves, we rely heavily on these unseen forces. We can move effortlessly through the world, yet always connected to the internet and one another. Similarly, nature is largely composed of fields – birds use them to migrate and whales to find their way in the vast ocean. Physicists have defined nature as composed of fields and particles. Certain *Laws of Nature*, such as magnetic fields, gravity, waves, and subtle energies of the Sun and Moon constitute a whole realm of fields that structure our universe.

We live in a field of consciousness that we don't often acknowledge. We do know that invisible environmental conditions affect people's behavior, health, and happiness. We feel stress, and we feel happiness. We are sentient beings who love the energy of life. Building *Enlightened Real Estate* is the method for intentionally creating a positive field effect within the built environment.

The atmosphere of the great city-states is well-known and appreciated. But what creates that "field" of feeling and energy? Is it the people and the geography or the buildings and the plan of the city?

In 1865, Scottish Physicist James Clerk Maxwell published *A Dynamical Theory of the Electromagnetic Field*, which demonstrated the existence of magnetic and electrical fields. This notion of understanding a physical phenomenon as a "field" made up of many separate-yet-connected things was new to scientific thinking. Since then, the concept of a "field" has become a commonplace idea in math, science, and popular literature.

Each person constitutes an invisible field of physical, emotional, intellectual, and spiritual energy. Each person influences the environment around them. A community is a field made up of many people. A community of stressed-out individuals feels a lot different than a community of happy, healthy people.

Individuals build communities; communities build cities. Each city has a unique collective consciousness, a distinctive flavor generated by the consciousness of its citizens and the quality of its built environment. This atmosphere that we feel, but do not see, is this invisible field of human energy interacting with the surroundings. In this way, Dubai is different than Paris, and Shanghai is different than Los Angeles. For example, the reason people come to New York City is for its unique atmosphere created by the intense economic and cultural activity. Everyone contributes to, and is in turn influenced by, the collective consciousness of the community.

As our own consciousness expands, it creates a ripple amongst the people around us. As more people gain access to the inner field of transcendental consciousness on a regular basis, the entire society will begin to spontaneously benefit. A more coherent collective consciousness creates greater harmony, bliss, and an atmosphere that minimizes problems and maximizes successes.

Buildings are the silent contributors to the field of collective consciousness of the city. Therefore, how, where, and what we build matters. They create part of the overall field that we experience. The interaction of humans and the man-made environment combine to make up the collective experience. It is people living, working, and interacting

50

with the built environment that forms the field effect that is the sense of place we call home.

CHAPTER 11
LIGHT AND THE BUILT ENVIRONMENT

"In the whole universe there is nowhere to be seen a body of greater magnitude and power than the Sun."

Leonardo da Vinci, 1452-1519

The Sun is not only the dominant energy source on Earth, it is also the principal influence on human beings and the buildings they inhabit. Throughout history, the rhythms of the Sun have regulated our daily routine and seasonal activities, such as planting cycles, travel schedules, and celebrations. In the past, buildings were often designed to take advantage of the transit of the Sun.

For many thousands of years, fire provided the only other source of warmth and illumination. In the late nineteenth century, that suddenly changed. New sources of energy were developed that could produce artificial light and heat. The first central power plant in the United States, Thomas Edison's Pearl Street Station, began generating electricity in 1882. In 1887, oil was discovered in Pennsylvania.

Once humans were no longer dependent on the natural environment for heat and light, buildings could be designed without regard to the Sun and other natural elements. This loss of connection to the environment has brought forth a whole host of unexpected consequences.

THE TRANSITION FROM SUNLIGHT TO SCREEN LIGHT

In 1929, Vladimir Zworkin invented the first transmission and reception system for television images. By 2015, there were two billion TV sets around the world.

The first, mass-marketed personal computer came out in 1977. By 2015, the estimated number of PCs was one and a-half billion worldwide.

The first call made on a cell phone occurred in 1973. This

phone weighed two and a-half pounds, featured a talk time of thirty-five minutes, and required ten hours to recharge.

In 2007, the iPhone was introduced by Apple, featuring the first practical touchscreen. In 2015 alone, Apple and Samsung sold over four hundred million smartphones.

The typical young person in the U.S. spends an average of eleven hours a day looking at screens. **This phenomenon has occurred over the last five years as more people make the transition from sunlight to screen light.**

The consequences of lives lived in screen light, rather than sunlight, are beginning to surface. Many people are spending upwards of eighty percent of their time indoors. The use of corrective lenses has skyrocketed, and attention spans have dramatically decreased. Time spent working or playing outdoors in nature has plummeted, and lack of exercise has affected our health. Sitting is the new smoking.

This separation of human beings from sunlight is an unprecedented development in human history. Social skills and interpersonal behaviors developed over thousands of years of civilization are being disrupted by a culture that has begun to think that the virtual world is more interesting than the physical world.

The psycho-physiological effect of long-term exposure to screen light is not widely understood. However, there have been many years of research on the various effects of colored light on plants and animals.

All life on Earth depends on sunlight. Sunlight is composed of ultraviolet, visible, and infrared wavelengths of electromagnetic radiation. Through photosynthesis, the Sun's energy is converted into chemical and molecular energy, which is the basis of plant growth and our food chain.

In the 1950's, while cinematographer John Nash Ott was photographing time-lapse sequences for nature films, he discovered that varying the colors of light dramatically influenced the growth of plants. **His experiments led to the understanding that only full-spectrum, natural light promotes good health in plants, animals, and humans.**

"My studies have indicated that light is a nutrient, similar
to all the other nutrients we take in through food, and that
we need the full spectrum range of natural daylight.
This is a fact long since proven by science. In 1967,
a paper presented by three Russian scientists to
the International Committee on Illumination said,
'If human skin is not exposed to solar radiation
(direct or scattered) for long periods of time,
disturbances will occur in the physiological equilibrium
of the human system. The result will be functional
disorders of the nervous system and a Vitamin-D
deficiency, a weakening of the body's defenses,
and an aggravation of chronic disease.'
That's the condition I now call malillumination, a lack of
the necessary amount of sunlight, just as malnutrition
is a lack of the proper nutrients in our diets."

John Nash Ott, Early Light Researcher, 1909-2000
Mother Earth News

SUNLIGHT'S INFLUENCE ON THE BUILT ENVIRONMENT

The modern phenomenon of overexposure to screen light could be remedied by building according to vastu architecture. A properly conceived built environment naturally exposes people to sunlight in the course of their daily routine. Furthermore, this vastu approach is more natural and cost-effective than trying to mimic sunlight artificially.

The Sun is a critical influence in our lives by creating the circadian rhythm of day and night. From dusk until dawn, the Sun supplies subtle energies that interact with our nervous system, enlivening various levels of awareness and wakefulness. For example, the morning Sun striking the kitchen helps stimulate digestion and alertness.

Vastu architecture recommends that buildings face east or north. As the Sun transits a vastu home, the various rooms receive different qualities of light throughout the day, helping one to study, relax, sleep, eat, or meditate. We may notice that certain rooms seem to favor activities in any house. When the rooms are misaligned, one may feel like sleeping in the living room, being awake in the bedroom, or eating in the den. The influence of the room placement and light quality can impact the physiology in either a positive or a negative way.

When our cities, homes, and daily routines are better aligned with the energy of the Sun, it leads to better health and well-being. This type of Ayurvedic daily routine[1] can lead to success in many areas of life, just as the famous proverb says: "Early to bed, early to rise, makes a person healthy, wealthy, and wise."

Improving our physiology through the correct influence of sunlight can be a significant factor in enlivening our outer well-being and inner awareness. Sunlight, in its all-pervasive nature, is the symbol of inner light, and consciousness is often referred to as the "light of life."

"What if we were made of light instead of dust...?"

Secrets of the Sun, Millennial Meditations

---

[1] For more information about the ayurvedic daily routine, visit: www.enlightenedrealestate.com/ayurveda

CHAPTER 12
CONSCIOUSNESS: THE ULTIMATE TECHNOLOGY

We use technology to locate friends, find a mate, communicate, design and build things, do research, be entertained, and buy products. As it turns out, the most powerful uses of technology are often those that touch deepest into our need to be loved, appreciated, and understood. Social media has become the new village market. People come to meet, gossip, flirt, make friends, and purchase goods.

Simultaneously, the way we use everyday products and services has been altered by technology. Consider the elegance of Apple products, the wonder of the Tesla electric car, and the convenience of Uber. You could swear it's your neighbor rushing over to give you a ride!

While human beings have had hundreds of thousands of years to evolve, the technological and cultural changes we've experienced in the last century constitute a major challenge to our physiology and the environment.

The velocity of change inherent in today's 24/7 world requires the constant checking of emails, social media, and text messages. While it connects us in virtual reality, it has the side effect of creating miscommunication and isolation in the real world. We are becoming habituated to this disconnected, detached feeling. Everyone is walking around in his or her own little digital universe.

This disconnect is causing a major reaction in the collective consciousness. People are searching for a way to reconnect to themselves and to the world around them. As an example of the changing trends, the millennial generation is introducing a new set of priorities: care of one's body, friends, community, and spiritual growth, all while developing purpose and passion in their lives.

The intense interest in real estate today is a direct reaction to the destabilizing influence of technology on the emotional and spiritual nature of human beings. The

built environment is the grounding, balancing, and connecting influence necessary to offset the impact of technology on us.

Houses are not solely a place to live, but also create a sense of belonging and a protective shield for family life. Office buildings should be built to encourage productivity, collaboration, and wellness. Communities should serve to connect people and give them a common identity. Shopping should be a community experience rather than a race through the supermarket.

> *"Modern transportation and technology have greatly speeded up life. We are asked to react almost instantly to both requests and opportunities. Life seems more unpredictable, harder to manage and stabilize.*
> *We often feel like we're missing out on something.*
> *The news reports, the uncertainty of the economy, instability in family life, climate change, all introduce more fear and uncertainty.*
> *A good regular daily routine can help a great deal in calming this uncertainty and fear. The practice of Transcendental Meditation and yoga, plus a more calming, serene, and stable home environment, like those available in a vastu home, can contribute to a calmer, healthier, and happier life."*
>
> *Dr. Sophie Beall, M.D., Ayurvedic Physician*
> *Maharishi Ayurveda Health Centre, Seelisberg, Switzerland*

Rapidly expanding technology has so drastically increased the demands on us that many people feel a deep intrinsic need to turn within. As the frontiers of innovation in every field get pushed further into the subtler realms of the material universe, we arrive at the final frontier: the inner world of human consciousness.

THE SINGULARITY?

Futurist Ray Kurzweil has predicted that by 2045 the technology of the day will exceed human comprehension and control. He has labeled this moment in history "The Singularity." Computers will be able to design and create themselves. Their computational capacity will dwarf the super computers of today. The consequences of this potentially paradigm-altering development have alarmed leading contemporary thinkers. What is missing from this theory is the uniquely human capacity to access the infinite reservoir of intelligence and creativity, the field of pure awareness, that resides within each of us.

If we rely solely on the intellect, we wouldn't be utilizing our full, innate capacity to experience reality; we would be denying our fundamental and natural connection to the infinite field of pure Being. This field of lively silence, which resides in each of us, contains within it all the *Laws of Nature*. This is the very spring from where intuition and genius flow, which forms the foundation upon which the human intellect is based. Computers will never have this ability because that would require them to be living, sentient beings. To build such a computer would be equivalent to building the entire human nervous system, which is inseparable from and unified with the universe and the intelligence by which it functions.

Finally, technology is simply incapable of experiencing emotions. The expansion of the human heart and the capacity to love creates more nourishing and powerful forces than any technology devised by man. No machine will ever be a substitute for the love a parent has for a child or for two friends sharing their lifelong experiences.

To ensure that we continue to be the masters of our technological and cultural destiny, we need to develop the consciousness of each individual. The combination of explosive technological growth, a built environment conducive to evolution, and the possibility of increasing self-awareness through meditation has the potential to produce a world of almost unimaginable prosperity, joyfulness, and bliss.

CHAPTER 13
OBSOLESCENCE CREATES OPPORTUNITY

*T*he obsolescence of traditional real estate asset classes is creating one of the biggest economic opportunities in history. Changing lifestyles, new technology, and the short lifespan of modern buildings all contribute to an excess of outdated properties.

We've spent the last hundred years building an impersonal, standardized society that can deliver products and services efficiently. Simultaneously, we created an isolated, suburban-based housing stock and office buildings that cater to individual businesses with minimal spaces for collaboration and innovation. The internet carries this trend to its apex. It has dramatically reduced the need for human interaction; everything is designed to be transactional.

Now the pendulum is swinging back to the local, personal, and unique. We want to have a real sense of roots, a place we contribute and belong to, where we can effortlessly connect with friends, family, and business associates. There is a migration towards this experience that is fundamental to our DNA: love, relationships, sharing, and togetherness. In every aspect of creation there is this interactive, interdependent quality. The digital universe is not a substitute for this basic aspect of our human nature.

The future of housing will take into account the changing lifestyle of families. Intergenerational compounds will become commonplace and provide a stabilizing influence on families. New types of construction, utilizing natural, environmentally-friendly materials, will improve health and longevity.

In the U.S., traditional malls and big box retail are substantially overbuilt. These asset classes have dominated the commercial real estate landscape since the early 1990's. Big box retail, including stores like Walmart, Target, and Best Buy, eliminated thousands of locally-owned stores around the U.S. However, just as big box retail took the world by storm with its grab-and-go stores, the internet has provided an even higher level of convenience by delivering the world to our doorstep.

The reality is that we still need a physical place to live, shop, study, and work, even if we spend much of our life online. We can't taste, touch, or smell anything on the internet, and we can't bump into our neighbors online. In office environments, the internet can't create the serendipity of ideas that flow when colleagues share thoughts over coffee. We live in the physical world and need spaces that help us evolve while accomplishing our goals.

People are drawn towards community-based stores as well as locally-sourced products and food. There is an explosion of community gardens and farmers' markets springing up everywhere. The Abbot Kinney neighborhood in Venice, California is just one example of a walking-friendly, small shop environment that has become a huge commercial success. The rise of the artisanal maker class shows our desire to connect to the local ecosystem.

New types of office buildings are being built to meet the needs of twenty-first century business. Co-working offices and live/work environments reflect the new way people work. Tenants are demanding workspaces where the windows open for health and energy-saving reasons. As the way we work changes, so will the spaces we occupy.

This next phase of the real estate market is a shake out, not a collapse. Well-located real estate will always be valuable. Obsolete assets and marginally-located real estate could be repurposed into *Enlightened Real Estate* developments that will provide excellent returns on investment.

THE NEW DIFFERENTIATION

A whole new approach is necessary to differentiate the developments of the future. Current tactics used to distinguish properties on the level of design, amenities, and starchitecture are becoming increasingly more challenging, especially in the ultra-luxury residential and Class-A office markets. With expensive marble, eccentric finishes, and flooring from rare sources, design has reached its limits of creating differentiation. When every new building has a pool, tennis court, gym, spa, dry cleaning, and childcare center, these amenities become the baseline expectation in the marketplace. As developers crowd into asset classes and the market reaches saturation, the limitations of design and standard amenities become apparent. The financial risk of overdevelopment is intensified particularly in the luxury market.

Luxury has always been the goal and symbol of an affluent life and is synonymous with the best, most expensive, and most exclusive of everything in the material world. It expresses the natural tendency of people to enjoy the expansion of life. Every great civilization has always reached for that aspirational goal.

Now, luxury is being radically redefined. The goal of unlimited golf, tennis, shopping, travel, and entertainment has recently merged with a focus on health and longevity. The next shift is towards a sophisticated lifestyle designed for the development of higher consciousness. **The biggest luxury is the time and technology to explore the inner Self, to be happy, healthy, and balanced in all aspects of life, and to live in an environment that is conducive to enlightenment**.

Ultimately, our experience of luxury depends on our inner happiness. The mechanics of perception is that there is a knower, what is known, and the process of knowing. The state of consciousness of the knower determines one's experience of something. A happy, balanced person will enjoy more. The more established in the Self the person is, the greater the ability they will have to find happiness in what they have. An ignorant person is often overshadowed by the object of perception. This is why people can be surrounded by luxurious things and experiences and still enjoy very little, while others can have very little and still find so much joy. The missing link in the process of enjoying the finer things in life is the state of the knower. An enlightened knower perceives the full range of experiences, and luxury will be fully appreciated in whatever form it appears. The knower will place a greater value on what they have in the material world. The ultimate experience is the full integration of the inner and outer values of life – which is the state of enlightenment.

This new definition of luxury is potentially available to everyone. Life can be reorganized for convenience and have a focus on health, togetherness, and the growth of consciousness. Everyone, from the ultra-wealthy to blue-collar workers and students, can start and end the day with meditation and live a low-stress, high-reward lifestyle. The luxury of evolution is that each person can progress each day, in their own way, and in their own time.

The new goal for real estate development is to create a holistic lifestyle to capture the experience of bliss and happiness that one feels in a state of enlightenment. Spaces should be designed to both the proportions and orientations of vastu to tap into the cosmic energy of the universe. The objective is ease, well-being, comfort, and balance.

New asset classes, such as the Ideal Village described in the next section, will be designed to fulfill the needs of this next wave of interest in spiritual development, health, and happiness. This transformation will require construction on a massive scale worldwide. Real estate is not only a vehicle for enlivening human potential, but will provide the stimulus for the next great phase of economic expansion. Only then can real estate reach its full potential and reflect our desire to create, grow, earn, love, learn, and evolve.

"Atmosphere is something that deepens over time. It's a relationship between the building and its occupants. The feeling you have in a building is from the collective energy of the people living, working, and interacting with the space. The new differentiation is a field of happiness that a properly designed building exudes."

Lindsay Scherr Burgess

SECTION 3

ENLIGHTENED REAL ESTATE
The Dawn of a New Asset Class:
The Ideal Village

CHAPTER 14
TRANSFORMATION THROUGH
RISING CONSCIOUSNESS

When we transform ourselves, we transform the world around us. As consciousness rises, people are becoming more aware of themselves and their surroundings. This is a catalyst for reimagining our man-made environment and ultimately our society at large. All aspects of the built environment will, by necessity, have to be reconstructed to reflect the needs of a community focused on enlightenment. As this transformation unfolds, the changes that we feel in our inner reality will come forward into the material world.

ALL THE WAYS THE WORLD IS CHANGING

The future has arrived. There are so many exciting changes happening due to the worldwide rise in consciousness. This is causing a transformation in virtually every area of life, including: personal development, energy, technological and scientific discovery, environmental sensitivity, organic food, cultural and artistic expression, business, education, transportation, and even real estate. We are already seeing examples of individuals living in more harmony with the Earth while utilizing the best technology available to solve the challenges we face.

ARTIFICIAL AND COSMIC INTELLIGENCE

Contemporary thinkers have voiced concerns about the rise of machines as predicted by the concept of "The Singularity"– the moment in 2045 when computers will be doing things most humans cannot comprehend. What has been overlooked in this conversation is the dramatic rise in human consciousness. Human intelligence, along with general awareness, is skyrocketing. Instead of being a threat, the use of artificial intelligence will be experienced as a natural and helpful development to remove many mundane tasks from our daily lives. If machines take over these everyday tasks, there is more time and opportunity for humans to develop themselves and take on more complex challenges.

Just as self-driving cars are on the verge of becoming commonplace, computer-driven machines will become increasingly more useful in the home and workplace. Although these machines may eventually gain the ability to perform many intricate tasks, they will never develop the ability to intuitively synthesize and analyze the millions of subtler variables that are necessary to advance civilization and understand the world around us. We have within us a universal, intuitional intelligence that spontaneously taps into the vast, infinite possibilities of nature. There is a difference between the intellectually-based skillset involved in the computation of specific information and formulas, versus the wisdom necessary to bring health, happiness, and world peace to humanity.

Thousands, if not millions of people whose consciousness is rising, will join the great thinkers of today. The combination of both highly-developed human awareness and powerful technology will help us create an ideal society.

EMERGING BUSINESS MODELS FOR A NEW ERA

We are now witnessing the rise of business models that emphasize design, community, and interconnectivity. Over the past fifty years, we have seen our economy cycle through a variety of boom and bust sequences, the crash of 2008 nearly bringing down the worldwide economy. The cure for this seesaw tendency is to create an economic foundation based on people-centric principles that encompass the full range of human needs and potential. Greater awareness and overall well-being allows one to more easily navigate economic fluctuations.

A business culture that simultaneously supports the development of human consciousness and economic

progress is the foundation for a stable economy. Full employment, not subject to a crisis every five to ten years, is only attainable when we base our financial thinking on deeper values. The most fundamental principle is to refocus on the welfare, education, and evolution of our citizens.

The complexity of today's worldwide economy is beyond any single intellect to fully comprehend. Therefore, we need to develop the full potential of every individual, thus creating a sufficient pool of managers better able to intuitively understand how to create and maintain businesses that can flourish in the tides of constant change.

Businesses need to recognize this new challenge as an opportunity. Trying to resist change will result in even the strongest, oldest, and wealthiest institutions failing because, as the pace of evolution accelerates, stress will quickly build up in any organization that tries to hold back the natural course of progress.

A more rested awareness increases the ability to adapt. As consciousness rises, one becomes more able to assess challenges and bring forth creative solutions. As Albert Einstein said, "We can't solve problems by using the same kind of thinking we used to create them." This rise in consciousness will create a new paradigm for mankind – and many new business opportunities.

Sharing has become cool. Uber, Airbnb, even ways to rent out one's power tools, are part of a new sharing economy. It's the new way to ask your neighbor for a cup of sugar or to borrow their shovel when it snows. The internet has opened up a new resource for fulfilling one's needs.

Services providers have become dominant market forces:

- Top Media Company: Facebook, creates minimal content

- Top Transportation Company: Uber, owns few cars

- Top Retailer: Amazon, has very few stores

- Top Hospitality Company: Airbnb, owns no hotels

Those who embrace the newly emerging culture of change will reach new heights of economic success. They will lead us into a new era of prosperity.

> *"With all emphasis, it should be stated that unless a man achieves a state of happiness of a permanent nature, he will not be contented and satisfied in life. To bring about this state of permanent contentment is the final aim of economics. Therefore, it appears that the field of economics should not be restricted to material production and consumption alone, but should be expected to bring about the means of greatest happiness of a permanent nature in everyone's life."*
>
> Maharishi Mahesh Yogi
> *Science of Being and Art of Living*

EXPANDING THE NOTION OF FINANCIAL SUCCESS

Even the notion of what constitutes financial success is about to undergo a major transformation. Finances will be seen as one component of wealth. The inner riches of enlightenment will provide a true basis for contentment, stability, and the ability to enjoy the pleasures of life. The way in which one makes money will also matter more than it does today.

The modern syndrome of being consumed by financial matters will be offset by the balanced perspective of more enlightened individuals. This will allow for all facets of wealth to be more fully enjoyed. The goal of economics should move beyond activity for the sake of activity to a more uplifting, restful way of life.

300-YEAR HOMES

Imagine a society that eliminates the need for most young families to take on thirty-year mortgages, thus freeing up billions of dollars of disposable income and millions of hours of time for other creative pursuits. The yardstick for analyzing economic expansion and progress has to move beyond pure math and take into account a wider definition of economics. Construction and renovation are a major component of job creation and economic expansion. Fueling this trend are homes that are designed to last one generation and require frequent renovation. This new paradigm will create a new type of housing stock that encompasses natural, energy-efficient, vastu, and intergenerational housing, called "300-Year Homes."

Houses that last for generations create a different dynamic. 300-Year Homes establish history and continuity for families that over time foster a sense of belonging that comes from being part of something bigger than oneself. By combining the flexibility and convenience of the American model with the stability and beauty of European structures, these homes will utilize the best construction principles to last far into the future.

ENERGY AND TRANSPORTATION

As we begin to shape our society in the light of higher consciousness, the way we build, use our energy, and move our people will be changed to a more environmentally-friendly and interconnected model. A consistent part of human history has been to underestimate the velocity of change once new technology arises. Why is it that there is currently fifty-times more power generated by solar and twelve-times more power generated by wind turbines than experts predicted by this time in history?

In the future, every community of one-hundred-plus homes will include a shared, sustainable power plant. Energy will be produced locally, with wind and solar plants located in each neighborhood, supplemented by larger plants that utilize efficient technologies such as fuel cells. Eventually, an infinite source of clean energy – possibly fusion energy – will be developed to dramatically reduce utility costs and environmental impact.

The velocity of human interaction, which translates into economic activity and wealth, is influenced by the efficiency of our transportation systems. In compact cities like New York, it is possible to schedule five or six meetings a day, whereas in Miami, where traffic is heavy and public transportation is lacking, one may only complete two or three such activities daily. South Florida is a very successful, creative place, but the economy would be even better if people could relate to each other on the level of purpose instead of traffic patterns.

Transportation will be revolutionized in ways we are only beginning to comprehend. High-speed trains could dramatically increase reasonable commute distances, thus opening up many new housing markets. These trains will become the primary intercity mode of transportation, eventually replacing the use of airplanes for trips of less than one thousand miles. Airplanes will run on biofuels or electrical energy and will be built of extremely light, but sturdy, materials.

Our love affair with automobiles is changing. With the advent of short-term rentals like ZipCar and Turo, and ride sharing services such as Uber and Lyft, car ownership will become an option instead of a necessity. The advent of self-driving cars will completely transform this relationship.

EDUCATION

As the nature of work changes, so does what people need to learn. Collaborative, project-based, internationally-focused education will better meet the needs of the future. Developing the ability to harness the genius that comes from greater consciousness into productive solutions for the future should be one of the main focuses of higher education. Universities, by their open source nature, will share research, ideas, and bring forth many amazing innovations. Molding tomorrow's innovators to be fearless, ambitious, and curious is crucial for our future success.

Ideally, all citizens would have access to continuing education programs that teach basic skills needed to function in our interconnected world. This would include subjects like citizenship, the arts, personal finance, advanced computer skills, foreign languages, social skills, meditation, and yoga. How we educate our citizens will determine the future of our society.

> *"The illiterate of the 21st century will not be those*
> *who can't read and write, but those who cannot learn,*
> *unlearn, and relearn."*
>
> *Alvin Toffler, Futurist, 1928-2016*

Students need to be able to increase their consciousness and tap into their true, unbounded potential. Through the regular practice of meditation, students will gain a greater capacity for understanding, learning, and synthesizing diverse streams of knowledge that make up this interconnected world. Not only will their stress level be reduced, but their coherence, confidence, and creativity will grow tremendously.

As an example, the David Lynch Foundation has implemented very successful school programs, called Quiet Time, where thousands of disadvantaged young people are being taught Transcendental Meditation. Young lives are being changed for the better. Programs have been implemented in San Francisco, New York, Los Angeles, Europe, and Latin America.

> *"Since I started TM, life has gotten a lot easier. I think*
> *more clearly and I don't rush into things. Plus, my grades*
> *have gone up."*
>
> *Cecilia, 7th Grader*

> *"When I meditate, I feel calm and like everything is going*
> *to be okay. I don't hold in my anger anymore or have*
> *outbursts of rage anymore. If more people learn, I think*
> *there will be less violence in the world."*
>
> *Elijah, 8th Grader*

CLOSING THE PHILANTHROPIC LOOP

Philanthropy is a natural instinct of the human heart.

Philanthropy can be a vehicle for helping to create an enlightened society. **To accomplish this goal, we need to close the philanthropic loop by crafting a system of giving that addresses the deepest reality of the origin of problems.**

The Medici family of the Italian Renaissance developed a model of philanthropy based on deep involvement with the kind of society they wanted to cultivate; they sought out and cultured genius, they created great civic structures, and they founded the Neo-Platonic Academy. It was the range of their vision that made their philanthropy a transformational force, which helped launch and sustain the Renaissance.

Renaissance Florence was considered the new Athens or Jerusalem of its time, largely because of the patronage and philanthropy of great families like the Medici. Today, we have the opportunity to create another Golden Age, a true Age of Enlightenment.

Philanthropy evolves just as civilizations evolve. The next step in philanthropy will be the organized collaboration among benefactors to curate an inspiring world, just as the Medici did. Meditation and yoga will be integrated into schools, prisons, and homeless shelters. Increased consciousness, better health, education, and inner contentment are the avenues for the disadvantaged to become permanently self-sufficient, productive members of their communities.

The reemergence of funding for beautiful public spaces as a point of convergence for the whole community will spur the construction of civic institutions such as schools, parks, art venues, and walking-friendly piazzas. The arts, which are crucial to a cultured society, will have dedicated funds, housing, and workspaces to support the next generation of artists. Neighborhoods of all socioeconomic levels will be revitalized by artists sharing their works in galleries, on the sides of buildings, and as public performances.

If we expand the goal of philanthropy to include the growth of consciousness and well-being, we move beyond the level of things we can see, to changes we can feel. This is the junction point between material and spiritual values that closes the loop and creates a never-ending cycle of benefits for everyone involved.

THE NEXT FRONTIER

We are beginning to fashion the world to support our journey to higher states of consciousness. **The next frontier is not outer space, it's inner space – the experience of the vast, infinite, and absolute world within each of us.** Our amazing species has the innate ability to not just understand, but personally experience the unified field of pure consciousness, a reservoir of creative, intelligent, blissful energy within us all.

As the outer, relative environment becomes increasingly more enticing and rejuvenating, our inner experience will also become more profound. Problems will just fade away. What ever happened to the Berlin Wall? One week it was there, and the next week it was gone. The physical world turns out to be quite fungible.

This goal is attainable. It is within our reach. We have the means and knowledge to accomplish this kind of existence for ourselves, our loved ones, and our worldwide community. As the collective consciousness rises, we will spontaneously become more and more aware of the underlying unity of all life, and a practical vision of an ideal society will gradually come into focus.

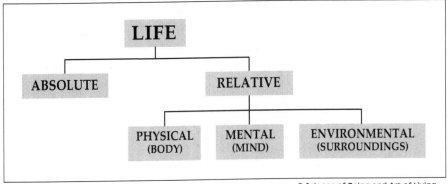

"The two main aspects of man's life are the relative and the absolute. The relative aspect of life is perishable; the absolute aspect is imperishable. The relative life has three aspects: physical, mental, and environment; or, body, mind, and surroundings.
Thus, we find that man's whole life has four different components: Being, mind, body, and the surroundings."

Maharishi Mahesh Yogi
Science of Being and Art of Living

CHAPTER 15
THE EVOLUTION OF REAL ESTATE

The built environment is consciousness expressed in matter. It is the clearest expression of an idea from its conception to its physical reality. Every piece of land starts as a blank canvas, and slowly over time, spaces are crafted based on available building materials, lifestyle, and the consciousness of the time. As we move forward and create new homes, buildings, and communities, how we structure our real estate will define our way of life.

As an underlying foundation of society, residential and commercial real estate are two of the biggest economic engines in any economy. Although it is commonly understood that a good economy is necessary for the real estate sector to flourish, it is not fully appreciated how the *quality* of the built environment affects the success of business and society at large. During this Economic Age, real estate is considered as a marketplace of space. Questions like, "How big is your house?" and "How many square feet is your warehouse, shop, or land?" are commonplace.

In residential real estate, space has always been a status symbol. This idea has accelerated in the Economic Age, driven by the need for self-identification in an impersonal society. People are defined by their address, square footage, or acreage.

In commercial real estate, space has taken on a generic quality. It could be reduced to an equation; twenty-five employees require "X" amount of space. Cost is often the major deciding factor. For example, this location needs this many square feet in order to place this much merchandise, or this many cubicles, etc.

The past fifty years have been characterized by the rapid rise and fall of various asset classes. This instability has become an accepted part of real estate investing. Today, there are a number of trends emerging that are giving rise to better long-term value for real estate investors. According to renowned Florentine professor Alberto Giuntoli, "In Italy, we build with the mindset that buildings and cities should last for generations." Today, there are initiatives to mimic the walkable, human scale design of the antique city centers of Europe that have maintained their value generation after generation. However, the ancient knowledge of building in accord with nature has largely been forgotten. The surging interest in LEED-certified, resource-saving buildings and biophilic design will propel a twenty-year redevelopment or retrofitting of properties around the world. There will be increasing use of architectural systems such as vastu architecture, which improves the well-being and consciousness of its occupants.

Real estate will begin to be looked at as a more intimate part of the equation that defines what makes business and community work. We inherently know we like some spaces better than others. Usually these preferences are defined by natural light, proper ventilation, design features, cleanliness, and overall atmosphere. On a more subconscious level, it is the emotional attractiveness of the space that influences its desirability and value.

As our consciousness grows, our feelings about boundaries shift – we can feel imprisoned or liberated by the world around us. Boundaries can be defined by the rooms in our homes, the walls in our office buildings, family structures, our ability to succeed in our career, or how we perceive ourselves and our culture. However, the most obvious boundaries are those of the built environment.

There is a movement away from boundaries of the impersonal, standardized, disconnected, and boring towards beauty, interactivity, creativity, connectivity, and walkability. Every asset class is going through an evolution to mirror the new lifestyle generated by increased consciousness.

REAL ESTATE OVERVIEW

What is the origin of the built environment we have?

Developers build according to their expertise, zoning and financing restrictions, market demand, and how they are used to earning their return. Let's look at the stages of the past, present, and future of the various property markets over the last fifty years to understand the trends.

RESIDENTIAL

1 Past: Suburban – After World War II, the suburbs exploded as a safe haven from the noise, crowds, and violence of the cities. The rise of separate households and idyllic suburban life became the ideal. Endless, curvy cul-de-sacs and indoor malls became the norm. Long commutes to the city for work clogged up roads and highways.

2 Present: Urban – The Baby Boomers' children grew up, and now they are fleeing the suburbs for the cultural stimulation, work opportunity, walkability, and convenience of city life. The high cost of living, overcrowding, and competition have led to a rise in stress.

3 Future: Multifamily Ideal Village Concepts

Planned Ideal Village Developments – This is a ten-acre-plus development with amenities for both the Village and the community at large. It will include a central piazza for community gatherings, an organic grocery store, child-care, elementary school, retail, restaurants, and community dining, as well as a clubhouse with exercise, yoga, and meditation rooms. The development will have both single and multifamily housing types to accommodate people in various stages of life. By meeting or exceeding the requirements of future generations, the Ideal Village is a new, self-contained development concept that will never go out of style.

Work/Live/Create Spaces – These are work/live lofts with an interactive design, including common work, dining, and recreational amenities. It is the ultimate convenience that streamlines daily routine, and creates a highly collaborative, work/live incubator space for creative professionals.

Ideal Village Compounds – This is a minimum one-acre compound where family and friend groups reside. It is an opportunity for shared common areas and responsibilities. Furthermore, the buildings will be completely self-sufficient with solar and wind power, rainwater harvesting, and built from extremely efficient and durable natural materials.

OFFICE

As people and technology evolve, the way we work changes, as does the workspace we occupy. The evolution of office space is as follows:

1 Past: Strict Boundaries – Traditional office spaces were separate and siloed. Cubicles were common, while community space was limited and often designed without the benefit of sunlight and outside air. There was an ego-driven desire to have a corner office for recognition, reward, light, and comfort.

2 Present: Reducing Boundaries – Offices are designed to encourage collaboration and innovation around complex tasks. Current design trends include spaces for learning, collaboration, socialization, and focus work. Walls are literally coming down, and many people are working in open desk formats. Open kitchens function as meeting and collaboration spaces. The inner core includes small alcoves for focus work and private meetings, allowing light to flow throughout the office. Sleek design is crucial to this concept.

3 Future: Unboundedness – The space will be designed to create both balance for the individual and greater stability and profitability for the company. This is the highest ideal for work environments, in which proper placement and proportion are used to create superfluid, inspirational spaces.

Work spaces will not be limited by traditional titles, but

rather allow people to flow from space to space based on their project requirements. Offices will be enjoyable, uplifting places to be. Cloud-based technology will allow teams to be productive anywhere, while low-cost, high-tech video conferencing will facilitate international collaboration. Fresh air and significant natural light will be two major factors in the space. Yoga and meditation rooms will be available, as well as a full kitchen for cooking. The combination of these elements will help create an alignment between the goals of the company and the interests of the individual.

RETAIL

The activity of being together in the context of purchasing one's daily necessities is deeply ingrained in our human DNA. If retail addresses this inherently personal experience, then it will continue to be an integral part of the commercial real estate landscape.

1 Past: Privately-Owned, Neighborhood Retail – Small merchants were the historical owners of neighborhood stores and open-air markets. Each store was fully customized for the local community. The success of the business was dependent on the individual entrepreneur. Service and personal touch justified the price point of this kind of retail. The advent of the automobile weakened neighborhood retailers by expanding the customer's mobility.

2 Present: Chain Store Era – In a movement towards efficiency and greater volume, corporate big box chains and malls expanded. Various retail concepts – from pet stores to electronics and office supplies – specialized in a category and dominated through price wars and variety. Walmart and Target have replaced many locally-owned businesses for everyday purchases. The massive industrialization of Asia has been intensified by the immense demand for cheap goods for these big box stores. As cost and volume have become the major deciding factors for the design and creation of many of these products, originality and quality have been compromised. The temporary, relatively inexpensive nature of products has introduced a consumption-based mentality.

3 Future: Integrated Retail – The velocity and diversity of commerce has increased dramatically. With the introduction of the internet, the way consumers procure products and services is changing. New innovations in online ordering, delivery, and a growing variety of products are disrupting the marketplace. For the first time during the 2015 holiday season, more shopping happened online than in brick-and-mortar stores.

The pendulum is swinging back to neighborhood living and shopping. Bricks-and-mortar, particularly neighborhood retail, will continue to thrive by providing services and entertainment conveniently, as well as offering spaces for new uses such as yoga studios, juice bars, artisanal shops, etc. Supermarket centers have been particularly resistant to the threat of online shopping. *Enlightened Real Estate* is a whole new category that will unite the neighborhood, people, and commerce into a joyful daily experience.

HOSPITALITY

Hotels suffer from an outdated idea of their mission. The next opportunity is to create a hotel that helps enhance the travel experience by expanding the consciousness and well-being of their guests. Travel has gone from a unique event to a frequent necessity. This change in lifestyle means that hospitality has to satisfy the need for total convenience, luxury, and wellness.

More than any other asset class, hospitality suffers from a lack of differentiation. The difference in physical amenities for three- to five-star hotels have become much less pronounced in recent years. Service and design remain the benchmarks of luxury. Simultaneously, there is increasing competition from Airbnb and VRBO.

Traveling should be a way to discover the world and oneself. Traveling opens new horizons, and hotels should be a vehicle for this. Hotels are gradually accepting, but not fully embracing, new concepts and activities such as healthy juice bars, nutritional breakfast options, yoga classes, aromatherapy, and spa-like showers, etc. Traveling should be a restful break from routine, instead of a frenetic, rushing inconvenience. Business travelers should be welcomed into a relaxing, rejuvenating space to help them recharge and be more productive. The purpose of the hotel should be to provide a home-like atmosphere that immediately calms the agitating effect of travel.

LOCATION, LOCATION, LOCATION?

The concept of location is considered a fixed reality, only modified gradually by time, new construction, renovation, or societal trends. We identify prime locations as areas where the action is – a city center or a main cultural or shopping area. Historically, a location's value has been based on commerce, transportation, amenities, schools, and demographics. If a property was poorly located, it suffered, and little could be done to change the area. Marketing, public relations, and brand affiliation are three tools that developers and Community Redevelopment Associations (CRAs) are currently utilizing to modify the value of their projects or certain neighborhoods. The Porsche Tower, Fendi Château Residences, and Armani Casa are three examples of condo projects in Miami Beach deploying these tactics successfully.

The evolution of real estate demands new ways to add value and differentiation to a project beyond what is being done in the marketplace today. We instantly know when we walk into a place that is beautiful and uplifting. There are visible characteristics: luxurious, human-centric design, peaceful indoor/outdoor spaces, enhanced common areas, walkability, piazzas in the center of planned communities, natural materials, etc. The invisible, felt atmosphere of a place is a tremendously overlooked aspect of real estate design. What if that could be consciously curated? The sum of this beautiful feeling and design, working seamlessly together, creates a sense of place and a special, attractive quality.

Vastu architecture creates an invisible, yet palpable energy field that supports the connection between the everyday reality and the subtler levels of life. Rising consciousness enlivens wealth and harmony in any community or city. The premise is that a building or community can become a draw, despite its location, due to the "vibration" or feeling it emits, and the collective consciousness it radiates. Minimizing the tyranny of location can unlock massive wealth by allowing new areas to grow and prosper.

There is a parallel revolution taking place in all fields of human and scientific endeavor. As we discover subtler levels of creation, more refined technology emerges. For example, the Tesla, a totally silent and non-polluting car; inaudible communication in text and email; and in the case of architecture, when structures and consciousness converge, it creates an irresistible atmosphere that trumps location.

The enlightenment of the environment is created by infusing an underlying field of coherence into buildings and city planning, thus raising the consciousness of the people, while simultaneously addressing the everyday needs of the populace. It's not based on static perfection, but rather creating a field of evolution where the pace of progress brings joy and happiness. **The new motto in real estate will go from: "location, location, location" to "location, connection, and consciousness."**

Every aspect of our physiology and culture can be nourished by a built environment that seamlessly supports an evolutionary daily routine. From how we plan our cities to the way buildings are built, there is a tremendous opportunity to reconfigure the built environment for a higher purpose. The results are not only transformational for the occupants, but highly profitable for those who develop and build for the enlightened paradigm of the future.

CHAPTER 16
RETURN TO THE HUMAN SCALE
(MISURA HUMANE)

Italian Piazza

I love the energy of the street. I look at the couples passing by and see the love in their eyes, the private tenderness. I observe the workers and see their focused commitment. There are many different paces of life: rushing, meandering, and everything in between! It is an emotional, dynamic tapestry expressing the joy of sharing a common place, of building it stone by stone, and living there generation after generation. This timeless interaction is a living metaphor for how the universe functions. In that sense, the city is the structure that we have created to admire and enjoy the diversity of life.

The Author's Reflection on City Life

The human scale should be the basis for the proportions of the built environment. Unfortunately, almost every urban design decision in America since the 1940's has been based on the automobile. The human scale has been largely abandoned. Cars dictate the way our communities are designed and built and heavily influence our daily routine. City planners have finally begun to recognize the need to return to a human scale, walking environment. Car-centric cities create stressed, out-of-shape, and isolated populations. Walking environments create high levels of socialization, convenience, and a healthier citizenry.

The historical city centers in Italy were built before cars. The streets and buildings were designed on a human scale that encourages walking, maximizes interaction between people, and optimizes commerce as part of daily life. Piazzas, lined with shops and restaurants, create a central meeting place for the entire community, where children can play safely, and all generations intermingle. Artisanal markets, concerts, and other communal events are every-day occurrences in piazzas. Daily fresh food markets, the norm in many countries, are gaining popularity in the U.S. and spreading this ancient ritual of people gathering together around local, fresh food.

Florence, Italy, one of the top tourist destinations on Earth, has been increasingly overrun by vehicles. In 2014, the mayor decided to close down certain streets in an attempt to return the city center to its traditional rhythm. Via Tornabuoni, Florence's most elegant shopping street, was closed to vehicular access. Once the closure occurred, foot traffic and business increased dramatically.

Misura Humane generates a profound sense of place and a completely different atmosphere. Each citizen shares a feeling of familiarity and a sense of belonging, which has a unifying influence on everyone.

The suburban lifestyle in the Economic Age has been defined by an exhausting separation of planned daily activities. The walking, human scale villages and cities of the future will reintegrate the activities of daily life into one seamless, joyful, and connected way to live. Socializing, exercising, shopping, learning, and working all overlap and become part of an emotional and evolutionary tapes-try.

People prefer walking to driving when there is some-thing interesting to see, do, and enjoy. The daily routine of the Mediterranean lifestyle allows more time for walking and social interactions. Friendships and family relation-ships have an opportunity to gracefully develop over time.

Bumping into friends after work, while grabbing ingredients for dinner, should be the norm. Joy would increase by the sheer serendipity and ease of life. Daily errands would be transformed from a series of tasks to a flowing, integrated, fun celebration with more time for everything. The rushing around, racing-against-time mentality needs to be replaced by a lifestyle that is conducive to living in the moment. Time is transformed from a scarce resource to a vehicle for evolution and opportunity.

A properly designed built environment becomes a silent backdrop that meshes the divinity of the human experience with daily routine. **By building to the Misura Humane scale, the environment returns to its original purpose.** It restores local conveniences and commerce, it strengthens the love we have for a place, and it honors the human physiology by respecting its divine proportions.

Human scale streetscape in Bologna, Italy

CHAPTER 17
REVEALING A NEW ASSET CLASS:
THE IDEAL VILLAGE

*T*here is an awakening of consciousness, which demands an entirely new community and lifestyle experience. As our mindset, culture, and priorities shift, so do the spaces where we live, work, and play. Real estate developers and city planners are starting to understand the financial potential of creating real neighborhoods. The recent surge of mixed-use town center developments seeks to recreate our community-friendly past. The Grove in Los Angeles and the San Antonio River Walk are well-known examples.

Currently, developers everywhere are striving to build something unique and different. Amenities like clubhouses, restaurants, golf, tennis, and special designs matter, but they don't create the wholeness of experience a true community generates.

A beacon of *Enlightened Real Estate*, the Ideal Village is the cutting-edge development concept to rebuild our communities and cities. It is a vibrant, interactive, mixed-use walking environment with the highest level of customized convenience. What sets these Ideal Villages apart is that they are built according to the ancient knowledge of vastu architecture that creates a sacred atmosphere, finally addressing the consciousness component of building that has been missing for generations. They have a layout reminiscent of the human scale, historic city centers of Europe. This broader perspective on real estate development could help halt the boom and bust of asset classes and create real communities with greater long-term value.

Vastu architectural building principles, which are independent of any architectural style, link the occupants to the spiritual side of themselves thus creating a dynamic energy and environment. An Ideal Village is simultaneously restful and energizing, a sensory experience beyond the visual, and a place with a tremendous feeling of well-being and purpose. This is the ultimate amenity, which transcends all others, because instead of merely connecting people to their economic and social lives, these properties connect the individual to their essential inner nature.

OVERVIEW OF THE IDEAL VILLAGE

In the coming years, many parcels near major cities will be transformed into villages for people seeking personal growth, enhanced community life, and business success. The ease of daily life will be a main pillar of this kind of community, allowing for joy, creativity, and stress-free accomplishment to flourish.

Imagine if new Ideal Villages, Towns, and Cities could be intentionally built to provide interactive and stimulating environments that surpass the energy of the existing mega city-states like New York, Los Angeles, Shanghai, Hong Kong, Dubai, or London.

Young people and families are all seeking alternatives to the stress and high expense of city life. The living wage debate has been exacerbated by the unending rise in the cost of living in most major cities. The Ideal Village solution will deliver a higher quality of life at a lower cost. For businesses, the unique energy and convenience of the Ideal Village will be the ultimate amenity to attract top talent.

The Ideal Village will include Vedic architecture in the local design style, ample gardens, and a pure, peaceful walking and biking environment. The Village will feature organic agriculture, alternative energy, and natural, Ayurvedic health treatments.

The Ideal Village will have a variety of facilities for all stages and aspects of life. A variety of housing options will be available – from recent graduates living in communal, dormitory-style apartments to intergenerational compounds for larger families and friend groups.

If we zone for it and build it, we will see density in suburban areas go up five- to ten-times as extended families or groups move in together. This allows families and friends to share costs, common areas, chores, garden and home maintenance, etc. This will be a wonderfully emotional environment where children and the elderly occupy an essential role, perhaps even reducing conditions such as Attention-Deficit/Hyperactivity Disorder (AD/HD), Autism, and Alzheimer's. Life thrives when it is full of meaning, feelings, love, and belonging.

Along with business and medical offices, it will have daycare for children and the elderly, theaters, galleries, and museums. The Village will have a community center with architecture conducive to social interaction and celebration. It will also include optional communal dining. Regular art exhibits, concerts, and educational events will help provide a lively forum for being together.

This will be a low-stress environment with emphasis on free time, recreation, and well-being. This garden village will be a place where contact with nature is a part of every-day life. Self-development techniques such as meditation and yoga will help create a harmonious atmosphere.

The Ideal Village can be built as a stand-alone project or as a building block to create an Ideal City. Ideal Villages will not need to be constantly rebuilt. They will last for generations. Architects and planners who design such Villages will be creating a legacy for themselves and communities that set an example of real estate as a vehicle for enlightenment.

This Ideal Village will become a model for the world. The actual structure of the Village will be designed to help people manifest whatever they desire. It is a truly sustainable community, where the common thread is higher consciousness for the individual; healthy, happy, prosperous people sharing their everyday life; free from pollution, noise, and suffering.

"Almost every civilization on our planet promoted an idea of a city plan, palace, or temple reflecting the order or harmony of heaven. The master plans were based on a regular, rectangular grid oriented exactly with the cardinal directions. Aligning the grid of roads with the North and South Poles, as well as the Equator, connects life in every building of the village or city with the cosmic structure. Each city has its central park or square. These principles were also used in ancient Rome, but were forgotten over time, leading to the chaotic expansion of most cities."

Wojtek Skalski, Vastu Architect

UNIQUE CHARACTERISTICS OF AN IDEAL VILLAGE

1 Maharishi Vastu Architecture – Building in Accord with Natural law

Vastu reintroduces the principles of nature to man-made design. Bridge engineers work by strictly applying gravity and wind load to their plans. Airplane design requires applying the laws of aerodynamics. Cities and buildings designed in accord with natural law will usher in a new understanding of the built environment and its relationship to nature. Vastu architecture restores the connection between the individual, the building, nature, and the cosmos.

2 Historical City Center and Human Scale Development

Community life can be elevated by creating buildings and civic spaces with humans in mind. Life becomes more convenient and joyful, car dependency is reduced, and daily tasks can be accomplished easily on foot, bike, public transport, or a short drive. In the Ideal Village, the citizens will be more able to do what they *want* to do, rather than what they *have* to do.

3 Walkability

Walkability facilitates interaction and connectivity. In a walking environment, one sees people as they go about their day. Running into a friend or colleague on the street becomes an everyday occurrence. In a driving environment, everything has to be consciously arranged and organized. The tedious demands of constant scheduling reduce serendipity and spontaneity.

4 Village Garden Design

This type of design reintroduces the idea of the garden as an integral part of the community experience. This type of landscape facilitates the connection to nature and beauty, encouraging residents to spend more time outside. Prolific edible landscapes and fruit and vegetable gardens create a local and seasonal source of food.

5 Cutting-Edge Technology and Innovation

The Village will incorporate the latest technology into building design, including solar panels and other energy-saving innovations. Self-driving, electric cars will navigate the streets. Shared office space will encourage collaboration and innovation. Low-cost video conferencing facilities will reduce the need for business travel.

6 Spaces for Yoga, Meditation, and Ayurveda

Common areas for meditation, yoga, and Ayurveda will be considered essential amenities for the community. These are practices that transcend culture and religion, bringing people together on the level of the development of consciousness.

7 Connection, Celebration, and Art

A major part of the Ideal Village is uplifting its inhabitants to inspire them on a daily basis. Art, creativity, learning, and day-to-day interactions are a central part of living in an Ideal Village. Interactive communication theatres will bring the world of culture and art to one's door with virtual art openings, lectures, and celebrations. Roving troupes of artists, chefs, speakers, and more will travel to spread their creativity and inspire others. Public art will line the streets and decorate the piazzas.

8 Restoring Investment

The Ideal Village reestablishes the idea of multi-lifetime investing. The current short-term five- to ten-year investment horizon will become obsolete. The construction of new multi-generational, mixed-use buildings will allow these investments to adjust to future trends by adapting to different uses over time. Furthermore, constructing buildings with materials that will last for centuries is the ultimate environmental approach.

9 Restoring Wholeness

A house consists of individual walls, floors, ceilings, doors, and windows. It becomes a home because the whole is more than the sum of its parts. There is a feeling of safety, belonging, and happiness; a place where a family can live and grow together. Similarly, when all the individual elements of community life are correctly established, the community automatically becomes a vehicle for personal and collective health and happiness.

The Ideal Village is a new asset class where every prescribed element helps to address the full range of human needs, aspirations, and experiences. If an Ideal Village is built, but the water and air are polluted, no one would want to live there. If amenities and schools are too far away, that defeats the purpose. When these communities are built with all the Ideal Village components in place, a transformative field effect is created, reestablishing the connection of people to their home, community, and deeper Selves.

"When a house is properly established in vastu, it generates an influence of coherence, harmony, and peace. The effect is more pronounced when an entire vastu community is established."

Vastu Homes and Cities in Accord with natural law

The finest spiritual buildings have always been built to nurture the connection between the individual and the cosmos. Just as musical instruments are designed to make a certain sound, buildings and communities can be designed to create a feeling of belonging. The Ideal Village magnifies each individual's ability to fulfill their desires, thus reestablishing the value and wholeness of community life.

ENERGY CONSUMPTION AND LIFESTYLE

One of the greatest challenges to humanity is climate change caused by carbon emitted into the atmosphere. Estimates of future carbon use are based on the assumption that the western, car-based, heavy meat-eating, energy consuming paradigm will continue as-is.

Ideal Villages, by their design and energy-efficient structures, automatically encourage lower energy-using behaviors. The average citizen in the Ideal Village would use up to sixty percent less energy than their suburban counterparts. This is not about going back to a simple, idyllic past. It combines the best technology available with vastu principals to restructure a society that is environmentally-sensitive and still conducive to an abundant way of life.

The eco-friendly aspects of Ideal Village living include:

1 Vastu Principals and Passive Design

The buildings are designed to be energy-efficient and require the least amount of artificial light and heat necessary. Natural light entering the home is optimized to be integrated with daily activity. Cross breezes can be used during the temperate months for heating and cooling.

2   Garden Cities – Walkable Streets and Open Space

These Villages will contain abundant gardens and foster a return to the beauty of nature. These outdoor spaces will encourage walking and congregating. Green space also improves air quality and can be used for food production, while green walls and roofs add additional insulation and appeal. Extensive landscaping reduces the heat island effect.

3   Lifestyle Design

Lifestyle directly impacts energy consumption. The introduction and adaption of this walkable, vastu, amenity-rich environment will cause major improvements in the everyday life of the residents. When schools, offices, activities, and entertainment are all within walking distance, it changes the connectivity of the community, while naturally reducing car use. The piazza becomes the center meeting point of the town. This lifestyle design creates an ongoing symphony of human interaction.

4   Ideal Village Zoning

Building and planning today is a fragmented process in a world that is moving toward being more holistic. The Ideal Village Zoning (IVZ) eliminates the endless debate over traffic generation, density, parking, and allowable uses in new development or redevelopment. There should be an IVZ fast-track process. When obtaining permits is a major struggle for the developer, the ability to create an innovative, multi-use design is compromised. People get so locked up in the transactional process, they lose the overall reason for the project and its impact on the community and environment at-large.

5   Building Durability

The use of high quality, natural building materials, with the ability to easily modify the interior, allows for a three hundred-plus-year lifespan for buildings and homes.

6 Decentralized Power and Co-Generation

Local solar, wind, and geothermal micro-grids will be in each Village.

7 Smart Technology and Efficient Infrastructure

The Ideal Village includes the cleanest and greenest technology to reduce carbon emissions.

8 Multi-Modal Transport

Walking, biking, and electric cars are preferred. Parking will be strategically placed on the periphery.

9 High-Speed Trains

America needs a Manhattan Project level commitment from the government to introduce high-speed trains to the U.S. As proven by most European and Asian cities, trains are the most energy-efficient and convenient way to travel.

10 Localized Food Production

A healthy, organic diet is encouraged in the Ideal Village. To facilitate this lifestyle, a large community garden and optional community dining are integral parts of the design.

The Ideal Village represents a solution to the conundrum of dramatically reducing energy use, while offering a superior lifestyle that people truly desire. Governments should consider establishing designated Ideal Village Zones for new construction or redevelopment.

MAHARISHI IDEAL VILLAGE

The Ideal Village is the embodiment of *Enlightened Real Estate* as it offers the possibility of addressing the full range of human endeavor in one place simultaneously. If properly designed, every citizen can find a healthy daily routine and fulfillment of every desire in the context of the same

Village. The common goal is the evolution of the individual, which governs the overall design, yielding an experience that would transcend individual preference.

In 1993, Maharishi shared his vision of an Ideal Village in the following quote:

"If you are interested in knowledge, supreme knowledge of natural law will be available to you when you are here at the Ideal Village.

If you want to possess a level of intelligence that will never fail you and will always support your desires, the Ideal Village will provide that to you on both levels – understanding and experience.

If you want power, the gates of the infinite organizing power of natural law will open to you when you are here. As the Rik Veda says, "Brahma bhavati sarathi" – the infinite organizing power of natural law will be the charioteer of all your intentions and actions.

If you are searching for measures of prevention for perfect health, supreme knowledge of perfect health, bordering on immortality, will be available at the Ideal Village. If you are interested in the fountain of youth, such knowledge and practical programs will be available here.

If you desire real happiness in life for yourself and all your dear ones, the Ideal Village will provide unconditioned, pure happiness.

If you desire not to be tossed about by the ups and downs of different values of the economy, politics, religion, and social change, the Ideal Village will provide that level of awareness, that steady level of consciousness, which will turn every situation to your advantage, which will prove the situation to be in your favor, whatever it may be to others. At the Ideal Village, you will have available to you the knowledge to prevent all future problems and failures.

If you believe in the philosophy of "hard work for progress," the Ideal Village will provide you greater progress through less hard work – a principle of living that is well worth knowing. The Ideal Village will provide winning principles for every level of life, whether you're a retailer, wholesaler, or producer. If you are a banker who sits and desires all to come to you as you grant, or an investor who knows what quiet investing is – for you the Ideal Village will confirm this theme of a quiet investor for whom all the other levels work. This is mastery over the unified field of Natural Law, and the Ideal Village will give you this.

If you are religious, the Ideal Village will give you that essential experience which is sought throughout the path of every religion – the sweet fruit of religious life.

If you are not religious, but are looking for some reliable scientific approach to find a supreme purpose in life, the Ideal Village is here to provide it.

If you don't worry about the purpose of life and simply want to enjoy, the Ideal Village has an exclusive offer for you: better health, greater energy, and intelligence in a luxurious setting.

If you are interested in nothing, then unbounded, unmanifested, pure wakefulness, unbounded bliss, the ultimate expression of pure spirituality, will be available when you are here.

This Ideal Village offers freedom from fear – freedom from fear of crime, sickness, and suffering. Above all, the Ideal Village will provide our nation with an invincible armor of positivity and harmony."

———————————

The Ideal Village will eclipse any built environment now in existence by creating a field effect that develops the ability of the individual to live life established in Being.

ENLIGHTENED REAL ESTATE FOR THE NEXT MILLENIUM

The Ideal Village concept, designed to last up to one thousand years, creates an interactive experience of happiness, longevity, and evolution. The following model is suitable for five thousand or more inhabitants.

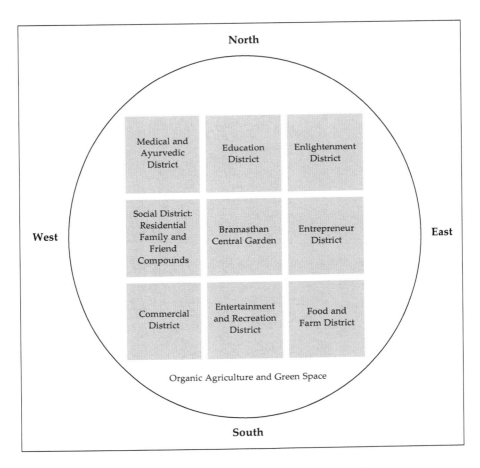

An Ideal Village is a collection of different elements – people, buildings, infrastructure, parks, streets, highways, public transport, etc. – that together compose the symphony of daily life. There are many characteristics unique to this Village concept, which when they are all integrated, will create a wholeness of experience and a harmonious atmosphere that is unprecedented.

A crucial differentiator is the use of vastu architecture in the design, construction, and planning of these Villages. As described in Chapter 18, vastu generates both stability and a cosmic aspect to the built environment. In some sense, vastu is the music, and the mayor – along with other civic, business, and artistic leaders – are the conductors. Just as concert halls are built to resonate music, likewise buildings and cities can be designed to amplify the energy and consciousness of their citizens.

Customized Districts will allow people to live in neighborhoods with others who share common hobbies and pursuits. These neighborhoods are all scaled to the human body and are walking-focused, in the sense that people can easily get to everything they need on foot, creating an irreplaceable intimacy and energy. This Village will be symmetrical on the grid with layouts that allow for easy navigation. Moving sidewalks, trams, and other light transport help people move effortlessly between the Districts. Vehicular access will be limited to electric or solar vehicles. Other vehicles will remain on the periphery for long distance trips outside the Ideal Village Zone.

The total effect of these elements is to create a cityscape that honors the physiology, emotions, and needs of each citizen. These Districts integrate art, commerce, medicine, sports, food, education, socialization, and the development of consciousness into every area of life in a seamless melody of daily celebration.

THE DETAILS

This concept will consist of nine Ideal Village Districts, all positioned on the NESW grid. Eight of the Districts will have a thematic concept, and the ninth is the Brahmasthan Garden District – a giant, special park with edible landscapes, benches, fountains, and lakes. It is a kind of Eden where the citizens can meet and recharge. This is a place where the purifying influence of nature meets the silent, absolute value of human consciousness.

The eight surrounding Districts will each be a square shape, and have a specific theme:

District One is the neighborhood for seekers of enlightenment. Like-minded people will gather here to enjoy yoga classes, morning and evening group meditation, healthy communal dining, and evening knowledge classes. Their daily routine will include all the aspects of life as in the other Districts – they just want to be immersed in as much spiritual bliss as possible.

District Two is the Entrepreneur's District. The special energy needed to create new, groundbreaking businesses will be the focus of this District. Incubator spaces provide cross-pollination of ideas. All the services young businesses need to thrive – including venture capital, lawyers, accountants, consultants, etc. – will cluster here to help ideas become reality.

District Three is the Food and Farm District – the food enthusiasts dream! There will be everything from daily farmers' markets and fields to grow fruits and vegetables, as well as herbs for medicine, to many restaurants clustered on the main piazza. Food workers, chefs, farmers, and their friends will choose this District in which to work and live.

District Four is the Recreation and Entertainment District. Every imaginable activity – from fitness to art to music, etc. – will be clustered here. People that love a vibrant cultural lifestyle may find this District the most attractive place to live. Additionally, convertible sports arenas will attract the best teams to play a wide variety of games and competitions. There will be special housing and workspaces for artists, filmmakers, writers, and musicians. District Four will also include an indoor and outdoor theatre and concert hall, which will have plays, films, exhibits, and concerts almost continuously.

District Five is the Commercial District. Shops, warehouses, and offices will be grouped together with homes located above the workspaces or nearby. Live/work lofts will be a popular choice in this zone.

District Six will focus on social life. It will consist of multi-generational, one-acre compounds for extended families or friend groups. The sites will allow for multiple buildings and up to twenty residents per acre. This will help with the easy care of children and elderly and create a warm and convenient family environment.

District Seven features a medical theme, including traditional systems like Ayurveda, as well as western medical offices and a community hospital. Doctors, nurses, and other health care professionals can easily walk to work from their homes and apartments clustered nearby.

District Eight will be the Education District. Teachers, professors, and researchers will especially enjoy living here. The District will have elementary, middle, and high schools, as well as a community college. This area will also encourage academic research and innovation.

Common Elements

Every great city gains its energy and uniqueness from a collection of different Districts or neighborhoods that express traditional areas of interest that people most enjoy. By concentrating activities into specific Districts within a Village, the variety of activities will bring new ideas and innovations as well as long-term success. Think about Broadway in New York – everyone gravitates there for some of the best theater on Earth! The special part of the Ideal Village Districts is that they are auspiciously located to maximize the coherence of the neighborhood and the synergy of the Village as a whole.

How would it feel if you shared many of the same interests as your neighbors or could easily reach every service that you needed for your business venture? Each District, through its common theme or activity, creates a field effect, a special atmosphere that inspires a shared community vision. Instead of solely organizing people by housing types, income levels, or zoning that separates living and working, this concept brings people together by their interests, goals, or professions.

Each District will have a central piazza with a giant fountain, marking the point of the brahmasthan. Each neighborhood will have access to a wide variety of shops, workspaces, and housing to help facilitate an easy daily routine. Many shared amenities, from common dining to childcare and shared car services, will ease the demands on individual households.

This is not an imaginary concept. It is the millennial vision for a daily life that is both blissful and purposeful. This is the safe haven investment of the future because it is a place that will flourish and remain valuable generation after generation. The variety of experiences available in the *Enlightened Real Estate* Ideal Village will integrate the expansion of happiness into all aspects of life.

CHAPTER 18
INTRODUCTION TO MAHARISHI VASTU
BUILDINGS AND COMMUNITIES

*"When a community is laid out and structured in
harmony with Natural Law on every level, the fortunate
inhabitants are destined to find health, wealth, success,
and happiness in their private and professional life."*

Dr. Eike Hartmann, Director
The Institute of Vedic Architecture and City Planning

Enlightened Real Estate means moving beyond shelter,
beyond short-term economic gain, to consider the stabilizing and potentially enlivening influence that buildings
and city planning can have. The most profound dimension
is the harmony and coherence that can be experienced
through the complete understanding and implementation
of this ancient science of vastu. This unique architectural system aligns the cosmic influences of the Sun, Moon,
planets, and magnetic fields of the Earth with human
beings by virtue of the structures we inhabit, thus connecting everyday life with the cosmic forces that administer the
universe.

In this age, physics is uncovering new subatomic particles and a deeper understanding of the unified field underlying all creation. Similarly, architecture is on the verge its
of own renaissance, once again realizing that an all-encom-
passing, coherent energy field is the most precious byprod-
uct of proper design.

According to the Vedas, complete bodies of knowledge
cognized thousands of years ago by sages in India, there
is a relationship between consciousness, the human physiology, the built environment, and the cosmos. This relationship is completely expressed by vastu architecture, also
known as Sthapatya Veda, meaning "the knowledge of
establishment." This ancient science of architecture offers a

fundamental technology to ensure the positive influence of a building on all aspects of the occupant's life.

> *"The ultimate truth is that we are cosmic Beings born of the same matter as the stars and that we are really cosmic inside, created in the image of God with a destiny to express his will on Earth as it is in heaven. Maharishi Vastu is the most ancient and supreme system of architecture and urban planning in accord with Natural Law, and offers the possibility of connecting and harmonizing the built environment to the Sun, Moon, planets, and stars, and the entire ever-expanding galactic universe, thereby connecting individual life with cosmic life, individual intelligence with cosmic intelligence."*
>
> Dr. Eike Hartmann, Director
> The Institute of Vedic Architecture and City Planning

Real estate constructed according to the principles of vastu design reintroduces the built environment as a stabilizing structure in society. Buildings become a junction point between the inner and outer realities of life. Buildings and communities create life-supporting influences as we go through our daily cycle of meditation, eating, working, studying, relaxing, and sleeping.

We need this deeper experience of inner silence, as expressed through the implementation of vastu architecture, as an antidote to the velocity and intensity of the modern world. Maharishi Vastu architecture ensures that a building or community will have only nourishing influences on its occupants by implementing several key Vedic principles and elements:

1 Right Direction

The orientation of a building has a dramatic and easily measured impact upon the quality of life of its occupants. The Sun's energy is most nourishing when it is rising. East facing buildings bring the greatest benefits to the health and success of their occupants.

2 Right Placement of Rooms

The Sun has differing qualities of energy as it moves across the sky. Vastu buildings are designed so that the specific activities that we perform within the various rooms of a home or building are aligned with the appropriate quality of the Sun.

3 Right Proportion

Proportion is a key to successful design in nature. Correct proportion and measurement in buildings strengthens the connection of our individual intelligence to cosmic intelligence.

4 Natural and Nontoxic Materials and Solar Energy

An important component is building sustainably with natural, non-toxic materials suitable to the local climatic conditions. This includes using materials such as wood, brick, rammed earth, and adobe; natural finishes such as clay stucco, marble, ceramic tile; natural fiber carpets, curtains, and furniture; as well as non-toxic paints and glues. Solar energy is preferred.

5 Other Important Influences

- Land slope
- Land shape
- Unobstructed rising Sun
- Influences in the environment, including bodies of water
- Auspicious timing for the commencement of construction

SPECIAL ELEMENTS

Maharishi Vastu buildings feature several unique elements:

1 Brahmasthan

Many structures in nature have a silent core of intelligence, and the activity of the structure is arranged around this core. We see this in the structure of galaxies, solar systems, cells, and atoms. This core is called a "brahmasthan," or the place where wholeness resides.

As in many structures in nature, there is also a brahmasthan in a vastu building or Ideal Village. This element helps the property to resonate with the cosmic structure of the universe.

2 Vastu Fence

Since these buildings are designed to be in harmony with the universe, the influence from the structure naturally extends into the landscape, providing greater protection and coherence beyond the front door. A vastu fence or wall marks the extension of this influence. Its proportions and measurements are set according to the ancient formulas of Sthapatya Veda.

3 Kalash

The kalash, a Vedic form installed on the roof of a structure, is a signature element of this unique architectural system. Meaning "vessel" in Sanskrit, the kalash enlivens the connection of the building with the cosmos.

"Every form of nature is created by a specific quality of intelligence. Nature is using mathematics and geometric principles in the creation of every structure. This means every specific structure, including man-made structures, represents specific qualities of consciousness or intelligence."

Wojtek Skalski, Maharishi Vastu Architect

Vastu has many benefits, from good health to peace of mind and business success. People who live and work in vastu buildings and communities find that they:

- Think more clearly and creatively
- Make better decisions
- Are more alert and refreshed throughout the day
- Enjoy more restful and refreshing sleep
- Have more energy and less fatigue
- Feel protected by their home and community

"For me, as a Maharishi Sthapatya Veda architect, it is the greatest fulfillment of my profession to integrate the eternal, life supporting and powerful effect of Vedic Architecture with sophisticated and elegant contemporary design."

Dipl. Ing. Christian Schweizer
Independent Architect and City Planner

CASE STUDY:
MAHARISHI GARDEN VILLAGE
RENDLESHAM IN SUFFOLK, ENGLAND

Garden Village in Rendlesham

Founded in 2003 in Rendlesham, this development includes many of the elements of an Ideal Village. This community features many amenities needed for a peaceful, blissful, and evolutionary lifestyle. It has eco-friendly vastu houses and apartments, an Ayurvedic clinic, and a thirty-room conference and course center, known as a Peace Palace. The center offers a wide range of courses to develop higher consciousness, including instruction in Transcendental Meditation as well as revitalizing retreats.

This community is designed in the traditional style of the region and augmented by the placement, proportion, and orientation of vastu principles. The developers have utilized local craftsmanship and materials with a focus on sustainability and beautiful design. This charming village, located just five miles from the ocean, is surrounded by cultural amenities, including historical seaside towns, prominent country estates, and the internationally recognized Aldeburgh Music Festival.

The proximity to the coast, lack of industrialization, and access to London have made the area a natural haven for artists and musicians. There are ongoing seasons of music, literary, food, and cultural festivals throughout the year. Since it is a rural, agricultural region, the community has easy access to organic and artisanal food products. The Garden Village is a twenty-minute drive from the enchanting coastline and a five-minute drive to three thousand acres of untouched forests. It is a ninety-minute drive to Cambridge University and two hours from London.

This development represents a highly advanced implementation of *Enlightened Real Estate* principles. It is a successful integration of vibrant community life with the goal of higher consciousness. The developers of this project are making every effort to create a lifestyle that reflects the goal of enlightenment as part of one's daily routine. Surrounded by nature and the best of the English countryside, the Garden Village is an island of silent, coherent bliss, a refuge from our hectic world.

This Maharishi Garden Village at Rendlesham is the convergence of the elegance of the past, the convenience and technology of the present, and the aspiration of enlightenment for future generations.

Vastu Homes in the Maharishi Garden Village

Rendering of the Peace Palace

CASE STUDY:
MAHARISHI VEDIC VILLAGE OF CANADA
PHASE I:
THE RIVERFRONT PIAZZA AT NIAGARA FALLS

The Riverfront Piazza is the proposed first stage of an ideal community situated less than two miles from the Falls.

The Vedic Village is a toxic-free, green, sustainable, carbon-neutral, healthy place, providing a forum for entertainment, serenity, harmony, and support for all two thousand residents to find their spiritual growth toward enlightenment.

Riverfront Piazza Master Plan

"Leave your car behind, and enter a green, eco-friendly world — a human scale village where everything you need is accessible by foot; live healthfully in "fortune-creating" vastu buildings; enjoy world-class Ayurvedic health treatments; indulge in vital organic food and produce from our own gardens and greenhouses; participate in a world class program of international conferences and cutting-edge knowledge for success in every field of life; enjoy unparalleled fitness opportunities in a glorious natural setting; and participate in group meditation programs to experience the fastest growth to enlightenment, as you contribute to harmony in the community, invincibility for the nation, and peace for the world."

Marketing Brochure for the Project

CASE STUDY:
MANDALA VILLAGE
FLORIDA, U.S.A.

The developers of Mandala Village are committed to making a difference. It has been said that the majority of developers design and market projects by "looking in the rearview mirror." The approach to the Mandala Village's planning and design combines forward-thinking ideas with the significant goal of creating a new paradigm for community development.

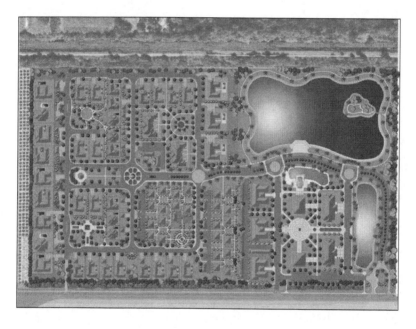

The Mandala Village Master Plan (pictured here) incorporates the principles of ancient Vedic town planning. Vastu is a tradition that is embedded in the deep understanding of the role that the proper structuring of physical space plays in creating a coherent and harmonious environment that supports peace, well-being, and happiness. Ancient town planning was always rooted in a deep spiritual appreciation of the value of community and the physical space that shaped it. Modern planning has been far too driven by a narrow, purely economic approach and a failure to embrace the deeper values that are part of creating a true community. Mandala Village combines both the practical and deeply meaningful aspects of community design.

The developer is proposing to build a mixed-use Traditional Neighborhood Development (TND) Community. The residential mix of the community will include a variety of housing types. The single family units include estate homes, mid-size homes (villas), and small courtyard cottages. Multifamily units will include townhomes, condominiums, and town center apartments over retail and office space.

The commercial mix will include a wellness hotel and spa, shops, offices, and a yoga and meditation pavilion. The community-specific Town Hall will include a dining facility that will be open to the public on a limited basis.

This project is being developed by Vero Mandala, LLC, under Richard Bialosky, A.I.A. and David Ederer.

CHAPTER 19
LA CITTÀ IDEALE
The Ideal City

Città Ideale. Dated 1480-1490, painter unknown. This work is likely inspired by Piero della Francesca. It is exhibited at Galleria Nazionale delle Marche in Urbino, Italy.

*A*s go the cities, so goes the world. The concept of heaven on Earth or Utopia has existed since time immemorial. It is a dream that has almost faded from our collective memory. Revived in modern times through Thomas Moore's *Utopia*, conceptualized in Pienza, Italy, and updated by the New Urbanism movement, it is the idea that the configuration and design of buildings can create community and even an ideal society.

The dream of an Ideal City is a Utopia where not everything is perfect, but rather a place where everything we need to evolve is provided. There is so much progress, and so few obstacles, that we feel we are living in heaven. We will have structured the experience of higher consciousness on the material plane, where one is able to create by intention. This aligns the physical daily life into a field of ease. Do less and accomplish more.

The Ideal City is a collection of Ideal Villages, which are neighborhoods that foster evolution from the transcendental to the emotional and the material. The Ideal City means a place composed of *Enlightened Real Estate*, multiple Ideal Village communities with fertile conditions for consciousness to grow in, and a context in which to enjoy full enlightenment.

THE RISE OF THE NEW CITY-STATE

Cities around the world have become victims of their own success. Today, fifty percent of the global population lives in cites. This number continues to increase year-by-year.

One of the biggest challenges is how to accommodate this rising population while maintaining and improving city life. The high cost of living, traffic, and pollution threaten the paradigm of the modern city-state. In recent years, many mayors have awakened to the fact that their city must nurture and sustain their population beyond merely providing jobs and encouraging economic activity. Due to the rise of these influential city-states, mayors have become among the most powerful people in the world.

We are in the midst of what is the biggest economic opportunity in human history – the rebuilding and restructuring of cities around the world. Therefore, the mayors are the key leadership for the next phase of economic expansion. This ongoing rebuilding activity will employ millions of people and reestablish cities as vibrant, opportunity-rich environments that keep up with modern lifestyle trends.

There is a reciprocal relationship between the city and its inhabitants. Cities express a viewpoint on reality that, in turn, creates an environment that supports or hinders its citizens.

THE CITY AS A COLLECTION OF IDEAL NEIGHBORHOODS

Greater Los Angeles has more than eighteen million inhabitants and covers 4,850 square miles. It is larger than Rhode Island and Delaware combined.

There are many village-within-a-city neighborhood areas of Los Angeles, such as Pasadena, Glendale, Silver Lake, Echo Park, Studio City, Culver City, Santa Monica, Pacific

Palisades, and Malibu. This revival of the village-within-a-city trend is accelerating because of widespread traffic congestion, inconvenience, and stress. More and more, people are realizing the benefits of village living, as it creates a neighborhood identity and roots within the community. Young people have discovered Venice Beach, California, as a place where they can live, work, and play in a contained, highly walkable environment. To reach their potential, these villages-within-the-city need to be rezoned, reimagined, and rebuilt on a livable human scale.

Some other examples of progress, in the direction of the Ideal Village, are taking place in the greater Los Angeles area:

CASE STUDY: CULVER CITY

In the 1990's, Culver City was an off-the-radar municipality nestled in the western portion of the Los Angeles megalopolis. Once the center of major Hollywood productions such as *Gone with the Wind* and *The Wizard of Oz*, it had endured a steady, slow decline since those glory days of the 20's, 30's, and 40's. Its main claim to fame was that it was the home of Sony Pictures Studios in the U.S.

The mayor and the city council – encouraged by Glenn Larkin, the owner of a newly-relocated upscale clothing retailer, and Frederick and Laurie Samitaur-Smith – joined forces to devise a strategy to revitalize the downtown. They worked hard to attract new restaurants, retailers, and a first-rate multiplex movie theater. They encouraged smaller, locally-owned business owners to set up shop there.

At the same time, many artists, musicians, and movie professionals discovered that Culver City offered the possibility of purchasing a house for a reasonable price. Within a few years, there was a large influx of these artistic people into the area surrounding the Culver City downtown area.

This once declining town has become a major destination spot. The LA Expo train line includes stops from downtown Culver City all the way to Santa Monica. Culver City

has now become a desirable place to live in Los Angeles –
a true success story and a great example of the need for a
village-type community.

CASE STUDY:
MID-CITY LOS ANGELES AND PACIFIC PALISADES

Rick Caruso is a Los Angeles-based, visionary real
estate developer who is moving his city towards a more
livable lifestyle. His landmark development, The Grove
in Mid-City Los Angeles, set a new standard for retail and
entertainment complex development. The Grove provides
a walking-friendly, small-town feel that is immensely
popular.

One of his next big developments is the Swarthmore
Avenue area of Pacific Palisades. This development will create another walkable, mixed-use environment within the
vast metropolis of Los Angeles.

CREATING AN IDEAL CITY

Here are steps to take in order to cultivate an Ideal City:

1 Generate a Strategic Plan with Key Stakeholders

A strategic plan is formulated by the mayor, county
supervisors, and city council in conjunction with the Committee of Three Hundred to designate Ideal Village Zones
within a city.

2 Form a Committee of Three Hundred

The Committee of Three Hundred is a concept designed
to activate community participation to create an ideal
society. Every city should consider having a Committee of
Three Hundred – a committed group of one hundred of the
city's most prominent people, one hundred experts from
all relevant fields, and one hundred concerned citizens –
who will work together to implement enlightened, collaborative solutions to the city's needs.

This Committee of Three Hundred would have a basic mission to encourage the development of the health, happiness, and consciousness of every citizen in all sectors of the community, while meeting the needs of everyday life.

3 Alter Land Use Through Alternative Transportation

These Ideal Village neighborhoods will become the primary economic generators of the city. Through the development of mass transit and the use of car-sharing and driverless car services, millions of acres of land previously used for parking would become available for other uses. The newly available land could be converted into various types and sizes of Ideal Village developments. They could be purely commercial, mixed-use, or residential.

4 Reduce the Cost of Living, Increase the Quality of Life

The cost of housing has now reached a tipping point within many major urban areas. The Ideal Village offers a new approach to this stubborn problem. Townhouses, condos, and multigenerational compounds, as well as small lot village environments with amenities such as common dining, childcare, and recreational facilities would offer a cost-effective environment in which to raise a family. The concept is to provide easy access for every imaginable daily need. The villages would become zones of commerce, safety, and convenience. One car households would be the new normal. By walking more, the health of the citizens would improve, thus incentivizing insurance companies to offer discounts.

5 Position Everything Within a Fifteen-Minute Radius

The city should be designed so that every home would be no more than a fifteen-minute drive or train ride from a village. This urban design would reinvigorate neighborhood commerce and identity. This layout would automatically rearrange the daily routine of its citizens. If each person spends less time in the car running errands and commuting, they will have more time for their family, friends, and the enjoyment of life.

6 Localize the Food Supply Chain

"Food is the new golf." Traditionally, planned communities were based on golf and tennis. Today, the hottest trend is easy access to local, healthy, organic food and fine dining. Very soon, food will be recognized for what it is: a basic component of a healthy, evolutionary lifestyle and a disease-free society.

The production of fruits and vegetables will be localized as much as possible. The utilization of organic practices and non-GMO seeds will be the norm. People will be appointed as "community farmers" and be responsible for the community's gardens and helping individuals to grow food on their private property. Cities and towns will donate land for these community gardens, encourage both front yard and backyard fruit and vegetable production, and plant edible trees in parks for people to pick. Backyard chickens and bees will also be permitted and encouraged.

The growing popularity of plant-based diets and relearning old techniques for growing, harvesting, preparing, and preserving food is a major cultural shift. Taking the time to enjoy our meals without rushing, as well as relearning to grow, eat, and prepare our food together is the next phase in nutrition.

7 Designate Artistic Zones by Revitalizing Underutilized Neighborhoods

Artists around the world frequently see potential in under-utilized industrial areas. They are attracted by low rents, large loft spaces, and reduced regulatory oversight. The growth of an artist community brings with it all sorts of auxiliary benefits: better restaurants, galleries, and stores.

The inevitable gentrification of these areas raises property values, and eventually the artists move out in search of new, affordable space. Artistic zones can be created by having zoning for live/work loft spaces where creative people can afford to live permanently. This maintains the creative energy force that is the basis of an original, vibrant, authentic city culture.

8 Create a City Identity Through Annual Festivals, Special Events, and Urban Retreats

In every city or town, there is a unique talent or product that distinguishes that place. By developing annual festivals, it stimulates the local economy, creates a unique identity for the city, and brings inspiration to the human heart. For example, Art Basel launched Miami as an international destination. In Italy, they have a wide range of food-based festivals. In Milan and Paris, they have Fashion Week. In the future, it will be consciousness-based events – citywide, week-long retreats for people to meditate and do yoga, with special speakers and healthy food, that will elevate the consciousness of the entire community.

9 Rethink Power Generation and Use

Today, the technology already exists to solve the majority of energy problems facing humanity. Solar power, wind power, and electric vehicles have been available for decades. Storage technology already exists, such as the Tesla Powerwall®, to help balance electrical supplies between peak and off-peak periods of demand. Yet inertia, habit, and special interests have delayed the implementation of these technologies. The widespread adoption of renewable energy systems will transform the urban landscape.

The old model of dependency on a central grid for power will be replaced by buildings that are independent, self-sufficient generators of energy and utilize the grid as a seasonal back-up source.

Modeled after the classic, historic city centers of Europe, these Ideal Villages will be designed with vastu principles and offer all the modern conveniences. With this in mind, the municipalities should provide subsidies for people who would like to tear down non-vastu buildings and build according to these parameters.

> *"We built America on the perception that there was endless land and limitless cheap energy. Our resulting lifestyle of excessive consumption and high mobility is spreading worldwide, and the capacity of the planet to meet our needs and absorb our pollution is being exceeded. Climate change is the most serious symptom of our unsustainable global economy. As Pope Frances recently taught in his Encyclical, we will need revolutions and transformations in our thinking and actions at all levels of society to secure our planetary home for our children."*
>
> S. Jacob Scherr, Former Attorney and Director of the International Program Natural Resources Defense Council (NRDC)

THE FUTURE IS NOW

La Città Ideale is not an abstraction, it's a full expression of ideal living. It infuses energy, love, consciousness, and happiness into everyday life. It brings to fruition the dream of Utopia as a field of consciousness that inspires our dreams and helps make them a reality.

CHAPTER 20
THE EVOLUTION OF THE AMERICAN DREAM

America is a country where dreams have come true for millions of people. Today, the new dream is to have interesting things to do, places to go, and people to see within the greater context of having a higher purpose. People are seeking the joy of community and the simple pleasures of just being together. The old dream of the isolated house on the hill has become a boring, lonely, and outdated way of thinking.

Around the world, a new generation of aspirational people is sparking a great awakening. This rising consciousness is expressed in a lifestyle that demands a new kind of built environment. The Ideal Village is the asset class of a lifestyle for personal evolution. This new form of community supports and enhances greater awareness, peacefulness, and well-being on every level. The Village adds the inner level of consciousness to the architectural equation.

The role of the builders and developers of real estate should be to build buildings that uplift the consciousness of their occupants. **This is the Ideal Village or City: a place where dreams can manifest because the fulfillment of desire is structured both in the consciousness of the residents and the design of the buildings.**

The American Dream is evolving, just like everything else in the universe. It is becoming something universal, something for the whole world. The American experience is the dream of breaking the boundaries of one's birth and aspiring to great achievement. Now a new lifestyle is emerging; one that is based on the idea of enlightenment as the most important and fundamental goal of our lives. We are each on our own unique journey of evolution to enlightenment. Each one of us should be born into a world designed and built for that purpose.

This will be the new dream of life on Earth, the new benchmark for accomplishment and luxury. It will be the

American Dream expanded to encompass the whole world being together in mutual respect and love. Our common humanity will predominate, and different viewpoints will become a source of strength and inspiration.

Why now, at this particular time, is there such a dramatic convergence of so many positive forces? Why are we experiencing an unprecedented explosion of knowledge and connection?

New technologies, as well as deep knowledge of the material world and the origins of the universe, combined with the revival of the ancient knowledge of meditation and yoga, has given us the possibility of rebuilding the world to reflect and nourish our highest aspirations. This is the American Dream reimagined as a universal dream for all humanity.

-CHAPTER 21
BUILDING A FOUNDATION FOR LOVE

What we build is a clear demonstration of how we feel about each other. Are our sole priorities commerce and privacy, or do they include beauty and connection? Do we continue to accept endless traffic jams, or make the effort needed to create great public transportation? Do we fear each other as dangerous "others," or do we see each other as potential friends on a shared journey?

No book on the built environment is complete without a discussion of emotions, love, and connection. The most important bridge is the one between each human heart.

We are attracted to that which brings us together, and fear that which tears us apart. The modern city is a jumble of emotions that stimulates the creative force. Meditation, yoga, and vastu will help enliven the *Being* part of being human. Otherwise, when life is filled with weakness and exhaustion, love will falter. When life is based on the infinite ocean of consciousness and self-awareness, it can thrive and grow from the deepest level of appreciation and recognition.

The way we see each other is deeply embedded in the physical expression of our homes, streets, public spaces, and even transportation. When we prefer the isolation of the automobile and the anonymity of modern life, when we insist on the illusion of separateness, then we establish loneliness rather than privacy.

The interactive nature of emotion needs a field on which to express itself. Love cannot flourish in too much solitude. We all need to live and interact with others to experience personal growth and to melt our differences. For instance, Italians inherently know this because beauty and love is the *raison d'etre* of their culture. Love and the expansion of the heart are natural responses to beauty. This impulse naturally arises from the consciousness of a happy, rested individual.

Life breathes love. Love fills the atmosphere with the unmistakable feeling that we are part of something bigger and more powerful than ourselves. That "something" is beyond the collective consciousness; it is the unified field of pure awareness, which is at the foundation of all experience.

The secret of life is our infinite capacity to love. This field of love provides nourishment just as important as food. It gives us the energy to reach out to find loving connections in relationships, business, and life. We recognize love when it comes and embrace it as the most sublime expression of who we are. Love exists to help guide and unite us.

Our home, our community, and our nation are the context in which we experience the love that guides our destiny. Life based on extended family, friendship, and love can transform the difficulties and inconveniences of the everyday into opportunities for more connection. We thrive when love can be found not only in the initial stages of intimacy, which is meant to be a fast-burning spark, but also in the long-lasting, steady fire that warms one's heart for a lifetime.

When we transcend the boundaries that bind us to the outer reality, then we arrive at the field of endless, divine joy. When we align ourselves with the Creator, we become an instrument of divine will, and our world becomes a living expression of one's higher Self.

The ancient buildings of the Renaissance in Italy still remind us of our potential to create beauty and express the divine in architecture, art, and music. When we enter a grand square or piazza, we feel a sweet togetherness. We have an immense ability to find the best in each other and to see and experience the perfection in our everyday surroundings. Architecture and art can be one vehicle for that connection.

The Ideal Village maximizes the openness, energy, and intelligence of its citizens. The human scale nourishes our feelings and supports our lives. The essential elements of natural food, clean air, and water ensure our health. The long-term success of the village and its inhabitants is much more likely when we acknowledge the entire range of human needs, emotions, and evolution. **We feel valued when we see our feelings reflected in the world around us.**

The body is the home of the soul, and the house is the home for the body. Vastu gives us the structure that reflects all creation and helps to connect the inhabitants to their own inner Being.

We are created in the image of God, and to rise to our true status, we need to transcend and reach that field of absolute creativity, energy, silence, and love that exists within each one of us. Enlightenment is born in this pure consciousness, cultured and enhanced by the group field effect, and accelerated by the nourishing qualities of the world around us.

When everyone in the realm of real estate embraces as their sacred responsibility the creation of places of love, then suffering will disappear from this world, as light dispels darkness.

CHAPTER 22
ENLIGHTENED REAL ESTATE

*Enlightened Real Estate represents the culmination of
mankind's search for meaning in the world around us.
Finally, there is a comprehensive reason for real estate –
the built environment as a catalyst for enlightenment.*

Rebuilding the world in the light of higher consciousness is among the most significant endeavors in human history.

It's time to bring real estate back as the great stabilizer
of society. Technology has interrupted the relationship
between human beings and nature. We have lost touch
with much of our connection to place. We have turned our
homes into investments. What was once passed from generation to generation has become a short-term storehouse
of wealth – monetized, traded, and often heavily mort-
gaged. We've traded stability for flexibility. However, the
pendulum is swinging back towards real estate as a way to
reestablish communities, institute new daily priorities, get
out of the car, and begin to create a way of life that is appropriate for a new time – The Age of Enlightenment.

The Age of Enlightenment means the inner value of life
is being acknowledged. There are two aspects of creation
that define our human existence: the unmanifest – the
infinite and unbounded level of pure consciousness
(inner) – and the manifest, relative world of boundaries
and expression (outer). Our physiology is unique in its
ability to experience both values simultaneously.

Until now, the outer, material-seen aspect of existence
has been the dominant experience of life. Still, we have the
innate capacity to experience the inner value of life through
thoughts, feelings, intuition, and ultimately the awakening
of our true nature. These two aspects, when fully integrated, create the wholeness of experience that is enlightenment.

THE REAL PURPOSE OF REAL ESTATE

"When the nature of the Self and the nature of the object are both shining, both in light, then that is the state of enlightenment. The Self in its full glory and the object in its full glory – two fullnesses, 200% of life."

Maharishi Mahesh Yogi

Creating communities that foster the connection between the inner and outer values of life is at the core of *Enlightened Real Estate*. Designed with the ancient knowledge of vastu, these communities will improve every aspect of one's daily routine, so that people walk, live, work, and enjoy in a zone of coherent bliss, grounded in their practice of meditation and yoga, and uplifted by the cosmic resonance of the buildings they inhabit. The infusion of the unmanifest field of Being into everyday life creates the effect of happiness, energy, intelligence, and organizing power.

Most people involved in the creation of buildings and neighborhoods have the sense that reconfiguring the built environment can change the world. Developers are already planning and building the communities of tomorrow to meet the emerging interest in well-being. Inspired by the antique city centers of Europe, the New Urbanism communities in America, and the younger generation's thirst for community, spirituality, and urban life, an awakening in real estate is already underway.

Today's increasingly high velocity of life requires a serene, established, and calming influence in order to withstand the intensity of change. It is critical that we skip ahead and move directly to building the neighborhoods of the future. This burst of enlightened redevelopment will be defined by simultaneously integrating all the elements of vastu, beauty, symmetry, connectivity, and convenience.

Rising consciousness will spark innovation, creativity, and true wellness – bringing in a new age of invention and prosperity. A balanced lifestyle will once again be possible, and work shall be as much for joy as sustenance. Education will be grounded in the Self, eliminating stress and encouraging exploration of both the inner and outer realities. Philanthropy will make major progress in meeting society's challenges and help us realize that our fundamental purpose is caring for each other. Love shall return to us as the emotional component of life that fosters togetherness and beauty. It is the catalyst for every transformation and the unifying force in nature. As a result, this new level of consciousness will bring new types of zoning, financing, construction, and insight into what constitutes proper planning and design.

The crowded life of the metropolis will gradually be replaced by thousands of new Ideal Villages of all shapes and sizes. These Villages provide the ultimate luxury – time – so that we can dedicate ourselves to enjoying life and developing our consciousness.

As builders, developers, mayors, planners, homeowners, seekers, and dreamers, we are actively involved in the way our society is shaped. As consciousness rises, we will choose to live in places that reflect who we are, and what we dream of becoming. This is *Enlightened Real Estate* – it inspires us, connects us, and lights up our world.

> *"One's knowledge depends upon the level of awareness with which one experiences the environment. Reality is different in different states of consciousness, and each view of reality is valid on its own level.*
> *There are two views of reality: one is that creation comes from the unmanifest, and the other is that the unmanifest never manifested into creation. These are two different states of consciousness, and each is true on its own level.*
> *In waking state of consciousness, one is completely identified with the objects of perception: the object is the only reality; the Self is non-existent.*
> *In Transcendental Consciousness, nothing exists but unboundedness.*

In Cosmic Consciousness, one experiences unbounded awareness, the Self, along with the boundaries of relative life. Unity Consciousness is the experience of Being as the source, course, and goal of everything. In this state of consciousness, one experiences the ultimate, unmanifest, unbounded, unified value of life."

Maharishi Mahesh Yogi
Maharishi Speaks to Students – Mastery Over Natural Law

CHAPTER 23

HOW TO BUILD MAHARISHI VASTU HOMES AND IDEAL VILLAGES

A SPECIAL SECTION BY JONATHAN LIPMAN, A.I.A.

"...A new world will be lived in by the same people. And what they will be? They will never be sick; they will never be shrouded with small things. There will be peace unbounded, prosperity unlimited, coherence unimaginable. This is vastu living."

Maharishi Mahesh Yogi
Building Fortune-Creating Homes and Workplaces:
A Unified Field-Based Approach to Architecture

I designed my first new community when I was twenty-nine. It was a heady experience to create something so large very early in my career. I used radical ecological principles in its design – the most progressive urban design theories of that era. I realize today that the most powerful environmental influences are cosmic influences, of which we are largely not aware. Wind, water, and solar gain are only part of this equation, but they are not the whole story.

I sentenced the families of that community to lives of less coherence and success than they might have otherwise lived. An urban designer's influence on life is enormous and extends for generations. The Vedic design principles that I have since learned have saved me from repeating the mistakes of my youth.

When urban designers first study the principles of Vedic town planning, they often ask me how a feeling of community connectedness is possible if houses do not face each other across the street. When I lived in Mandala One Village, located in Vedic City, Iowa, a Maharishi Vastu single-family housing development, I discovered that every evening one or two couples would step out of their home and go for a stroll in a loop around the community. As they passed other homes, I watched other couples step out of their homes and join them. Within a few minutes, I witnessed a small parade of neighbors chatting as they strolled together.

Such social phenomena, which occur spontaneously, are strands of the web that build a rich, truly connected community. The timeless Vedic principles of design are beyond human comprehension; they bring our lives into harmony with natural law in ways that we can't anticipate.

ELEMENTS OF MAHARISHI VASTU IDEAL VILLAGE DESIGN

Maharishi Vastu design brings the missing element to village design – a reliable way to create nourishing influences in the lives of its citizens: good health, happiness, success, and ultimately enlightenment.

It is alignment with natural law that brings coherent mental functioning, and from that comes a successful life. This system increases coherence in people by aligning the layout of homes and communities to the influences of the sun, moon, and North and South Poles. The principles of Vedic city planning are ancient, time-tested, and have been fully restored and systematized by Maharishi.

AUTHENTICITY

Vastu is the oldest and the most systematic of the world's architecture and city planning systems, but much of its information became fragmented or lost. As a result, as it is widely practiced, vastu is inconsistent and of diminished value.

Derived from his insight into the deep functioning of natural law, Maharishi recognized the potentially important, unique contribution of vastu to create success and happiness in individual life and harmony in society. He spent many years working with the foremost experts of Sthapatya Veda ("the knowledge of establishment") in India to systematically review and evaluate all the ancient texts. Maharishi unified and reestablished the practice into a fully effective system of architecture and urban planning.

This scientific, natural law-based system, is referred to as Maharishi Vastu or Maharishi Sthapatya Veda architecture. The preface of Maharishi in the title is used to give respectful credit for restoring this important system to its greatest wholeness and practicality, distinguishing it from from other vastu systems.

The system is taught in a rigorous post-graduate program to licensed architects, followed by an extensive internship, after which they are entitled to refer to themselves as Maharishi Vastu architects.

WHAT ARE THE KEY ELEMENTS?

Site Selection

The selection of the site for any building, development, or city is of primary importance. The texts of vastu record the various nourishing or harmful influences of these environmental elements, such as the slope of the site and the position of nearby bodies of water and hills.

Right Orientation

Maharishi Vastu planning places importance on right orientation to the east, the direction of the rising sun, which maximizes the natural life-supporting influence of the sun and the other celestial bodies. Natural law-based city planning orients all buildings to the east, or alternatively to the north, which has other life-supporting benefits.

In addition, the most successful city will be entered primarily from the east and north.

The Grid

In order to orient buildings to the east, the city plan must be laid out on a grid oriented precisely to the cardinal directions. This grid has an extremely important effect. Geophysics and astrophysics tell us that the Earth, like other celestial bodies, exhibits a variety of wave-like dynamics extending over the whole planet. Since the Earth spins from west to east on its north/south axis, there is a symmetry-breaking effect on the long-period surface waves, quantified by spherical harmonics. It implies that such wave-like dynamics generate a grid along the cardinal directions on the surface of the Earth. Buildings that are aligned to this grid naturally resonate with the dynamics of the Earth.

Proper Placement

As the sun traverses the sky from east to west, it generates different qualities of energy. In Maharishi Vastu architecture, these differing influences of the sun determine the ideal locations for the various zones of a city and functions in a building. Through this mechanism, natural law supports our activity.

Layout with a Silent Center – Brahmasthan

When we examine the structures of nature, we consistently find that they have a silent core. For example, galaxies have a black hole; solar systems have a star; cells, molecules, and atoms have a nucleus. We understand from Maharishi Vastu principles that this is a necessary element of a stable structure of natural law. In Sanskrit, the language of the Vedas, this element is called the "brahmasthan," the place where the wholeness of the structure is established. For cities to be holistic structures in harmony with natural law, they must also contain a brahmasthan. Within the grid of a Vedic city, this is commonly a beautiful central public square or garden. This element has been copied throughout the history of urban life; around the world we see gridded cities organized around a central piazza. Similarly, there should also be a brahmasthan within a building.

The Boundary – Marking the Vastu

On the selected site, properly oriented, and auspiciously proportioned, a vastu (a square or rectangular site delineated by a fence or wall, with auspicious entrances to the east or north) will be marked for the entire city.

This pattern applies also to Vedic buildings; the vastu fence, proportioned according to the mathematical formulas of natural law, establishes the property in relation to the environment, the community, and with resonance to the global and cosmic structure. When a building or house is properly established in the auspicious dimensions of a vastu demarcation, it generates quite a real influence of coherence, harmony, and peace.

Vedic Measurements and Proportions

Proportion and mathematical rhythm are familiar elements of design in nature. A unique feature of Maharishi Vastu architecture and planning is that the measurements and proportions of any layout or structure are calculated according to eternal, cosmic formulas. This ensures a perfect resonance between the cosmic structure and all components of human-made structures. Every part is thus connected to the whole in a way that promotes the health, wealth, and happiness of each individual, as well as the community at large. The design itself can reflect a local style to fit in with its surroundings.

Modular Master Plan System

Vedic city planning is composed of modular elements – the smallest is the individual building and its vastu yard; the next is a cluster of vastus that often corresponds to a city block; the next is a neighborhood of blocks centered on a brahmasthan; and these can be combined into larger units, until a city is laid out. An infinite number of configurations can be achieved with varying degrees of density and building types. The modular system allows for simple manipulation of the master plan over time, thus adapting to changing market situations or other unforeseen requirements.

Low Density

Ideal density is often exceeded in cities. The stress of individuals affects their neighbors. When a population is too dense, the accumulated collective stress contributes to disease, crime, and suffering. This is a principle of natural law that is commonly experienced. A successful city based on natural law avoids extremely high density and thereby produces an improved quality of life for its families.

Auspicious Timing

For special moments, such as ground breaking, laying of the first foundation for the village and every building, and the inauguration of a home or development, auspicious times are calculated according to Maharishi Vedic astrology, so that the full force of natural law will provide a maximum beneficial influence for the undertaking.

Materials and Technologies in Harmony with Nature

The advancements of the Industrial Age have begun to leave harmful marks on society and the planet. In response, humankind is beginning to appreciate the value of building in harmony with nature. In addition to using natural and non-toxic building materials, we also promote energy-efficient construction, and the use of sustainable utility systems, including on-site photovoltaic energy production, and other cost-effective, self-sufficient, non-polluting technologies.

A community is aligned with natural law through such

strategies as: positioning the roads to the cardinal directions in a properly-proportioned grid, locating community functions according to the inherent qualities of the zones of the grid, providing a central community square, surrounding the community with green buffers to reduce outside influences, laying out the community so buildings are oriented to the east or north, emphasizing the eastern entrance to the community, incorporating photovoltaic electricity generation to minimize levels of electrosmog, incorporating small-scale organic urban agriculture, and planting the community lushly enough that its residents feel that they are living in a garden.

A FEW STEPS TO INCORPORATE VASTU PRINCIPLES INTO THE DESIGN OF YOUR DEVELOPMENT

Here are a few simple steps to incorporate these principles into your next development project:

1 Our Maharishi Vastu architecture team will give you a list of auspicious and inauspicious site influences for you to consider as you look for potential project sites. For example, hills to the east of a site will block the nourishing influence associated with the rising sun, or a nearby high-tension line may not contribute to good health in the community.

2 As you identify possible sites, we evaluate them for vastu qualities before you commit to buying one. We can also evaluate a lot that you already own. We, or your urban designer in consultation with us, create a concept design of a vastu master plan to permit you to evaluate building density, infrastructure costs, etc. This will allow you to develop preliminary financials for the project and to solicit feedback from municipal authorities.

3 If you greenlight the concept and want to move forward, then we, with your civil engineer, develop the village master plan. In other cases, your urban designer takes the lead on the design, and we consult with them on vastu elements as the design progresses. As needed, this consulting will include concepts for some of the building plans, so the team understands whether the planned unit sizes and construction density work from the vastu perspective.

4 Building design may be done by your local architect, by us, or you may use our predesigns. If building design is by your local architect, then we will begin by giving them a detailed orientation of the major Maharishi Vastu building design guidelines, and we will consult with them as the project progresses in order to integrate vastu principles.

5 Optional: When the project is completed, a representative from the Institute for Maharishi Vastu Architecture can make a site visit to observe the buildings in order to award them with a certificate of compliance.

Maharishi Vastu architecture is a cohesive, precise, and holistic program to design buildings and communities that enliven and enlighten their occupants. It brings an influence of good health, happiness, family harmony, and success. Such Ideal Villages offer an unprecedented opportunity to change the way people feel on a profound level when they interact with the man-made environment. With this knowledge available, why would we build any other way?

CHAPTER 24
EPILOGUE
WHERE DO WE GO FROM HERE?

What if we could eliminate the fear in the real estate business by creating universally beautiful and timeless buildings for this generation that are easily adaptable over time? What if we could build a property that lasts forever? What if the first thing we considered when designing and creating buildings and communities was the balanced and happy daily routine of the residents living there? Imagine what would happen if we did everything right.

Every real estate investor, homeowner, and banker dreams of buildings that never go out of style, need no major renovation for generations, and everyone wants to live, be, vacation, or work there, independent of its location. This seems impossible and denies the *Laws of Nature* by which real estate currently functions. Times change, tastes change, habits change, transportation changes, and so the drama of rising and declining asset classes is part of a Darwinian cycle that favors both patience and flexibility. The Ideal Village resists the gravity of time and provides a unique solution to a long-term problem in the real estate business.

Every aspect of the human dimension, including its impact on creating a healthy, convenient, and evolutionary daily routine, will be the measure of real estate and will drive financial returns in the future. **Every paradigm has a beginning and an end – except for true human connection.** The impersonal lifestyle brought us *grab and go*, now we want to *stay and enjoy*.

The elephant in the room is the internet. It will not eliminate human nature, but rather create a thirst for real connection that will make Ideal Villages the safe haven investment for the future.

Artificial intelligence is one more attempt to mimic

nature. We already have that infinite potential inside of us, it is embedded in the structure of our physiology. We only need to tap into it, and then take responsibility for creating an ideal world.

We humans gather around a purpose that inspires us to action. Building for enlightenment is the next big wave in modern real estate history. *Enlightened Real Estate* is a trend that will propel a new way of life that reflects and expresses our deepest desire to connect to the world around us and to our higher Selves.

Enlightened Real Estate brings the light of pure consciousness into the field of matter. Building one thousand Ideal Villages in, and at the edge of, the great cities worldwide would transform the world.

When we rethink the purpose of life and the world we want to create, when our investment horizon includes future generations, when real estate is once again understood as a major catalyst for progress, we can seriously consider *Enlightened Real Estate* and the Ideal Village as the wave of the future.

How to proceed:
- Be aware of the evolution of asset classes
- Consider your mindset about the purpose of the built environment
- Notice the shifting lifestyle of the young and retired that is altering the real estate landscape at a velocity unknown in history
- Build a vastu home
- Build a vastu building
- Build an Ideal Village where you live
- Learn TM
- Contact us for a presentation about *Enlightened Real Estate*
- Visit EnlightenedRealEstate.com for photos and updated information

"Expansion of happiness is the purpose of life, and evolution is the process through which it is fulfilled. Life begins in a natural way, it evolves, and happiness expands. The expansion of happiness carries with it the expansion of intelligence, power, creativity, and everything that may be said to be of significance in life."

Maharishi Mahesh Yogi
Science of Being and Art of Living

SECTION 4

WHO, WHAT, WHERE, AND HOW

HELPFUL LINKS

Maharishi Vastu

maharishivastu.org
vediccityplanning.com
vastutv.com
www.maharishivediccity-iowa.gov
msvhomes.co.uk

U.S. Office Contact

info@maharishivastu.org

European Office Contact

vediccityplanning@maharishi.net

Transcendental Meditation Technique®

United States: tm.org or 1-888-532-7686 (LEARN-TM)
England: uk.tm.org

David Lynch Foundation Website

davidlynchfoundation.org

Maharishi University of Management Website

mum.edu

Maharishi Ayurveda Spa Treatments and Products

United States: theraj.com
U.S. Products: mapi.com
Switzerland: ayurveda-seelisberg.ch
Holland: meruhealthcentre.com
European Products: ayurveda-products.eu

Rendlesham Peace Palace (Conference and Retreat Center)

peacepalace.org.uk

THE TRANSCENDENTAL MEDITATION TECHNIQUE

"Know thyself" through Transcendental Meditation –
and with this knowledge you will have the power to know
everything, be everything, and do everything. Like the
hollow nothingness within the seed of a tree, which
contains the potential of the entire tree, the experience of
nothingness in the unmanifest field has within it the
lively potential of everything in creation. From that level,
you don't have to work hard to achieve anything.
You only have to desire what you want and
Natural Law will serve you. This is the knowledge
we want all of our children to enjoy – now and for all
future generations."

Maharishi Mahesh Yogi
Global News Conference, 2004

The Transcendental Meditation Technique is a simple,
natural technique practiced twenty-minutes, twice-a-day,
while sitting comfortably with the eyes closed. The TM
Technique is easy to learn, simple to practice, and is not
associated with any religion, philosophy, or lifestyle. Over
six million people have learned it worldwide, including
people of all ages, cultures, and religions.

The Transcendental Meditation Technique is thousands
of years old. It comes from an unbroken tradition of meditation instruction from ancient India. Maharishi Mahesh
Yogi first introduced the technique to the West over fifty
years ago. It was Maharishi's idea to subject the TM technique to scientific scrutiny in order to establish its practical
benefits for daily life. Maharishi has trained tens of thousands of TM teachers who are providing TM instruction in
all parts of the world. In a recent cover story on science and
meditation, Time Magazine recently credited Maharishi for
the revival of meditation and yoga in the U.S. and around
the globe.

The experience of the most settled state of awareness –

pure consciousness – through the TM practice produces a profound state of inner peace in individual life. This individual peace spreads naturally to the environment as well. Every individual influences his or her family, friends, neighbors, colleagues, and society as a whole, every day. Not surprisingly, if enough people are experiencing inner peace, then that peace can radiate strongly enough into the environment to influence social trends.

Fortunately, no belief or change in beliefs is required to learn and practice the TM technique – nor to gain all the benefits. In fact, you can be one hundred percent skeptical, and the TM technique will work just fine. This is because the technique makes use of a natural mechanism within the mind and body – long forgotten by most people – to settle down and take profoundly deep rest. No amount of belief or disbelief will change that inherent ability.

"People who come to me for relief from stress and stress-related disorders need an effective meditation that's quickly mastered and produces consistent results. Though TM is a mental technique, due to the mind-body relationship the practice has extensive physiological effects. TM allows the mind to settle very deeply inward – in a natural way. TM teachers call this effortless transcending. It's what sets TM apart and why the technique is so beneficial for mind and body, right from the start."

Dr. Gary Kaplan, M.D., Neurologist
NYU Medical School

INSTITUTE OF VEDIC ARCHITECTURE AND CITY PLANNING DIRECTORY

For more information, visit:
www.VedicCityPlanning.com

BOARD OF DIRECTORS:

Chair

Eike Hartmann
sthapatya@mac.com
vedicarchitecture@maharishi.net

Director for the U.S.A. and the Caribbean

Jonathan Lipman, A.I.A.
jon@jlipman.com

Director for Central Europe and Africa

Christian Schweizer
christian@maharishi.net

Director for Eastern Europe and Asia

Wojtek Skalski
wskalski@maharishi.net

Director for the Mediterranean and Latin America

Alberto Castano
sthapatyaveda@me.com

Director for Great Britain

John Renwick
john.renwick@naturalbuilding
design.co.uk.

Director for New Zealand and Oceania

Neil Hamill
nzsthapatya@gmail.com

Director for Australia

Meredith Lyons
info@vastuarchitecture.com.au

Director for Global Surveying

Roger Audet
vastu@maharishi.net

MAHARISHI VASTU BUILDING AND COMMUNITY PLANNING FOR NORTH AMERICA

United States: Jonathan Lipman, A.I.A.
For more information, contact: info@maharishivastu.org or (641) 472-7570.

Jonathan Lipman, A.I.A. is the Director of the Maharishi Vastu consulting service for the U.S., the Caribbean, and Canada. He is North America's leading practitioner of Maharishi Vastu architecture and urban design.

He has been practicing this nourishing system of design since 1996 and has worked on hundreds of Vastu projects, both buildings and community plans. He is an award-winning architect and a New York Times-praised author. He has guest lectured at Harvard, Stanford, and Yale Universities, as well as the Smithsonian Institution, the National Building Museum, and the Museum of Modern Art (New York).

Visit Fairfield, Iowa and Vedic City, Iowa – This is the greatest concentration of Vastu buildings in the United States and the home of Maharishi University of Management.

Visit www.MaharishiVastu.org for more information.

PEOPLE TO WATCH

1 Dr. Eike Hartmann, Jonathan Lipman, Wojtek Skalski, Christian Schweizer, and Alberto Castano – The Vedic Design team specializing in Maharishi Vastu Architecture
Visit: VedicCityPlanning.com and MaharishiVastu.org

2 Jeffrey Abramson – The Tower Companies built the first LEED Platinum, vastu office building in the U.S.
Visit: TowerCompanies.com

3 Craig Robins – Developer of the Miami Design District, a twenty-year redevelopment effort to transform an up-and-coming part of Miami into a high-end luxury shopping and artistic district
Visit: Dacra.com

4 Rick Caruso – Developer of The Grove, The Palisades, and many other walkable, mixed-use developments in California
Visit: CarusoAffiliated.com

5 Richard Bialosky, A.I.A. – Architect and Builder in Vero Beach, Florida with a specialty in Maharishi Vastu homes
Visit: NavoBuilders.com

6 Jonathan Burgess, PLA, LEED AP BD+C & ND – Landscape architect and planner with a background in sustainable design, development, and LEED consulting
Visit: ParadeloBurgess.com

7 Jonathon Phillips, Architectural Assistant – Studying and practicing Maharishi Vastu architecture at Maharishi European Research University and working on his RIBA accreditation to become a chartered architect
Contact: jonathongphillips@gmail.com

INSPIRATION

His Holiness Maharishi Mahesh Yogi

In 1955, Maharishi Mahesh Yogi began offering to the world the quintessence of the timeless wisdom of the Himalayas. He began to teach the simple, natural technique of Transcendental Meditation, which allows anyone to experience and utilize the source of infinite intelligence and creativity within ourselves – the field of pure consciousness. This effortless and systematic technique had been lost to human life until it was brought to us by Maharishi, inspired by his own teacher.

During his life, Maharishi worked with scientists, educators, and advocates of ancient Vedic wisdom to develop an integrated approach to this knowledge in the fields of science, medicine, and architecture. He wrote many books and circled the globe numerous times, speaking with world leaders and lecturing widely. In 1971, Maharishi founded Maharishi International University (later renamed Maharishi University of Management) and developed Consciousness-Based education, so that students could discover the field of pure consciousness within themselves as the source of all knowledge. My humble and deepest appreciation to his Holiness Maharishi Mahesh Yogi and the tradition he introduced to the modern world.

Dr. Tony Nader, M.D. - Ph.D.

Dr. Tony Nader received his M.D. degree from the American University of Beirut, where he also studied internal medicine and psychiatry. His Ph.D. is in the area of Brain and Cognitive Science from the Massachusetts Institute of Technology (MIT). He was a Clinical and Research Fellow in Neurology at the Massachusetts General Hospital, Harvard Medical School, and Assistant Director of the Clinical Research Center at MIT. His interest in the full potential of the human mind led him to the practice of Transcendental Meditation (TM), and he soon began working closely with Maharishi.

Dr. Nader has successfully correlated each aspect of the Vedic Literature to a specific area of Human Physiology – anatomy, cells, and DNA – with the conclusion that human physiology is the expression of Veda and the Vedic Literature. He is an author of a number of books on this topic. Dr. Nader's brilliant explanation of how our physiology is an expression of consciousness is a profound gift to the world.

In appreciation for his achievements and profound knowledge of both Vedic Science and modern science, Dr. Nader was honored by Maharishi with the title 'Maharaja Adhiraj Rajaraam' and given responsibility for guiding the Global Country of World Peace, the umbrella organization for all of Maharishi's worldwide legacy.

SOURCES

Richard Bialosky

Richard Bialosky, A.I.A. is a recognized leader in the field of green building and green community development. Mr. Bialosky has been practicing architecture and actively engaged in real estate development for over thirty years. Over the past two decades he has received over sixty national, state, and local design awards. Over the course of his career, Mr. Bialosky has developed over 1,500 residential units, as well as many commercial and office projects. He is currently involved in the development of homes and communities in Vero Beach, Florida – combining the age-old principles of Vedic architecture, non-toxic, health-promoting construction protocols, environmental sensitivity, and an emphasis on planning techniques that promote a sense of community.

He is on the executive board of the Treasure Coast A.I.A. Chapter and a member of the newly formed City of Vero Beach Architectural Review Committee. Mr. Bialosky resides in Vero Beach, Florida with his wife Jane. Information about Mr. Bialosky's project can be found in Chapter 18.

Dr. Sophie Beall, M.D.

Dr. Beall is the Medical Director of the Maharishi Ayurveda Health Centre in Seelisberg, Switzerland. She is renowned in Europe for her knowledge of Ayurveda, an ancient form of Indian medicine with a focus on preventative health. She is also a medical doctor, with a specialty in Pediatrics, Family Medicine, and Public Health. We interviewed Dr. Beall, and her quote is included in Chapter 12. To learn more about the Health Centre, visit: www.ayurveda-seelisberg.ch.

Dr. Eike Hartmann

Dr. Hartmann is the Chairman of the Board of Directors of the Institute of Vedic City Planning and Minister of Architecture for the Global Country of World Peace. He worked directly with Maharishi to bring forth the lost knowledge of Sthapatya Veda architecture to the world. By interviewing the foremost Vedic experts in Vastu Shastras ("the science of architecture"), the Sthapatyis of Ved Bhumi Bharat, they reestablished the purity of Vedic architecture, the fundamental principles of Vastu Vidya ("knowledge of dwelling"). He edited the book *Vastu Homes and Cities in Harmony with Natural Law*. He is the CEO of the Fortune Creating Homes company in the Netherlands. He has a doctorate in Vedic Science from the Maharishi Vedic University in the Netherlands. He is also a professor at the Maharishi University of Management in Fairfield, Iowa. Dr. Hartmann's quotes can be found in Chapter 18.

Christian Schweizer

Christian Schweizer is a Maharishi Sthapatya Veda Expert. He is Director for Central Europe and Africa at the Institute of Vedic City Planning in the Netherlands. He studied architecture and city planning at the University of Stuttgart, Germany. Over the last fifteen years, he has designed and supervised construction for more than one hundred Maharishi Vastu homes, villas, as well as public and commercial buildings for many different clients. He is quoted in Chapter 18.

Wojtek Skalski

Wojtek Skalski, DSCI is a Maharishi Sthapatya Veda expert. He is the Director for central Europe and Africa at the Institute of Vedic City Planning in the Netherlands. Mr. Skalski has designed Maharishi Vastu buildings for Finland, Denmark, Norway, Sweden, Ukraine, and Poland. He is presently designing an Ideal Village in Denmark according to vastu principles. He currently resides in Finland and travels the world giving lectures on Vedic architecture. His quotes can be found in Chapters 14, 17, and 18.

The Vedas

Vedas are extensive, ancient bodies of text, translated from Sanskrit as "knowledge." The Vedas are considered cognitions by ancient sages, carefully preserved since ancient times. There are four Vedas: The Rik Veda, the Yajurveda, the Samaveda, and the Atharvaveda. This is where we derive our knowledge of meditation, yoga, Ayurveda, and Sthapatya Veda. References to the Vedas are found throughout the book.

John Adams

John Adams, Jr. was the second President of the United States, and Vice President under George Washington. As a Founding Father, he was known as a leader of America's independence from Great Britain, as well as a lawyer, author, and diplomat. His quote in Chapter 3 comes from a letter to his wife Abigail in 1780, while visiting France. He was studying the beautiful art and gardens of Versailles and talking about bringing such beauty back to the newly formed United States.

Jill Black

Jill Black is a philanthropist and real estate investor based in Los Angeles, California. She is also a Director of the Joyce and Stanley Black Family Foundation. She sits on the Board of several philanthropic organizations including the David Lynch Foundation, which teaches veterans, underprivileged children, and prisoners Transcendental Meditation. Jill graduated from The American University. She has two children: Zach and Torie Zalben. Her quote can be found in Chapter 8.

Jacob Burckhardt

Born in 1818, Carl Jacob Christoph Burckhardt was a Swiss cultural and art historian. He was born and lived his entire life in Basel, Switzerland, except for periods of study in Italy. He is known as one of the first to study the cultural history of Switzerland and Italy. Burckhardt's best known work is *The Civilization of the Renaissance in Italy*, first published in 1860. He also published: *Remarks about Swiss Cathedrals, Force and Freedom: An Interpretation of History by Jacob Burckhardt, The Age of Constantine the Great, The History of the Renaissance in Italy*, and *Der Cicerone: Eine Anleitung zum Genuss der Kunstwerke Italiens*. He is quoted in Chapter 3.

Winston Churchill

As Britain's most famous Prime Minister, Winston Churchill led the country from 1940 to 1945 and from 1951 to 1955. He was also known as a writer, historian, artist, and officer in the British Army. He served in many capacities in the British Government, and was well known for his work both domestically and abroad. He was married to Clementine, and they had five children. He died in 1965 at age 90. His quote in Chapter 1 is from a 1943 meeting at the House of Lords, discussing the rebuilding of the old Parliament building that was destroyed in WWII.

Leonardo Da Vinci

This Tuscan Renaissance man is one of the most well-known and revered artists, scientists, inventors, musicians, architects, and writers of all time. Born in 1452, he worked in Florence, Rome, Bologna, and Milan, producing works such as the *Mona Lisa*, the *Last Supper*, and the *Vitruvian Man*. He was part of the Medici's Neo-Platonic Academy of artists and philosophers. He also kept extensive notebooks, studying diverse fields and inventing many new technologies that would take centuries to be realized. His quote in Chapter 11 came from his notebooks full of his intense observations of the world and the cosmos.

Albert Einstein

Nobel Peace Prize winner, theoretical physicist, professor, and a participant in the Manhattan project, Albert Einstein has made many notable discoveries and observations about science and the universe. He is most famous for his mass-energy equivalence formula, $E = mc^2$, and his general theory of relativity, which is the one of the basic pillars of quantum mechanical theory. He was instrumental in discovering nuclear fission during the Manhattan Project. Born in 1879 in Germany, Einstein fled just before WWII and became an American citizen in 1940. During his lifetime, he published over three hundred scientific papers and over one hundred fifty non-scientific documents. He was affiliated with Princeton University until his death in 1955. You can read his ingenious quotes in Chapters 9 and 14.

Alberto Giuntoli

Mr. Giuntoli is an Italian landscape architect and a professor at the University of Florence in the Landscape Architecture Department. He has a Degree in Agricultural Sciences from the University of Florence. He also studied Plant Ecophysiology at the University of Essex (UK) and has over twenty years' experience in the field of green design. He is a researcher and consultant on environmental issues for various U.S. and Italian governmental agencies and the European Union. He is a member of the Italian Botanical Society, the Italian Society of Arboriculture, and the Tuscan Society of Horticulture. He is also a member of the American Society of Landscape Architects (ASLA). He has spoken at numerous Italian and foreign conferences, is the author of over forty scientific publications in Italian and international journals, and is the director of the oldest journal of Italian horticulture, *Bullettino della Società Toscana di Orticultura.* He is quoted in Chapter 15.

Ray Kurzweil

Ray Kurzweil is a prize-winning inventor, scientist, futurist, and author. He has won awards from MIT, Carnegie Melon, and the National Medal of Technology for his inventions. He is the recipient of sixteen honorary doctorates and honors from three American presidents. Mr. Kurzweil has written many books, including: *The Singularity is Near, The Age of Spiritual Machines, The Age of Intelligent Machines, How to Create a Mind: The Secret of Human Thought Revealed, Fantastic Voyage: Live Long Enough To Live Forever, Transcend: Nine Steps to Living Well Forever,* and *The 10% Solution for a Healthy Life: How to Eliminate Virtually All Risk of Heart Disease and Cancer,* all focusing on cutting-edge technological trends in the fields of medicine, artificial intelligence, and transhumanism. He lives outside Boston with his wife and has two grown children. More information about his predictions can be found in Chapters 12 and 14.

Dr. John Nash Ott

Dr. Ott was a photographer and cinematographer who developed time-lapse photography and full-spectrum lighting for home and commercial use. He was one of the first to study and experiment with different spectrums of light and their effects on plants, animals, and ultimately humans. His major discovery was that humans need full-spectrum light for optimum health. He is the author of several books, including *My Ivory Cellar* and *Health and Light.* He is credited with the following films: *Dancing Flowers, Secrets of Life,* and *Exploring the Spectrum.* He also developed and marketed the only artificial light that replicates the Sun's natural, full-spectrum of light. His quote in Chapter 11 is from the Plowboy Interview in Mother Earth News, January/February 1986 Edition.

S. Jacob Scherr

As a visionary leader in the international environmental field, S. Jacob Scherr has spent the last forty years as a defender of the most endangered and important places on the planet and as a crusader against climate change. As a Senior Attorney with the Natural Resources Defense Council (NRDC), Mr. Scherr served as Director of NRDC's International Program and the NRDC BioGems Initiative. He was heavily involved in the Earth Summits in Rio, Johannesburg, and Copenhagen. Most recently, Mr. Scherr organized an eco-art campaign, which lit up the Eiffel Tower during the COP21 meetings with impactful messaging about climate change. Mr. Scherr's important victory to save Laguna San Ignacio in Mexico against the construction of a giant Mitsubishi salt works plant was just one of the many BioGems campaigns he waged in the Americas. Mr. Scherr retired in 2016.

Mr. Scherr is a 1970 graduate of Wesleyan University in Middletown, Connecticut. In 1974, he received his JD with highest honors from the University of Maryland Law School. He is married to Carole, and has two children, Lindsay and Adam. His quote is in Chapter 19.

Christoph Thun-Hohenstein

Christoph Thun-Hohenstein is an Austrian lawyer and art manager, who spent eight years in New York at the Austrian Cultural Forum as a diplomat. His other posts with the Austrian Foreign Ministry include Abidjan, Geneva, and Bonn. He is currently the General and Artistic Director at the Museum of Applied Arts (MAK) in Vienna. He studied law, political science, and art history at the University of Vienna. He has written several books, and his quote from the Foreword of *Uneven Growth: Tactical Urbanisms for Expanding Megacities* can be found in Chapter 5.

Alvin Toffler

Born in 1928, Alvin Toffler was an American writer and futurist known for his observations on technology's impact on society. As a writer, he published thirteen books with his wife Heidi, most famously *Future Shock, The Third Wave,* and *Powershift,* and worked as an editor at *Fortune Magazine,* exploring cultural shifts in society. During his career, he founded Toffler Associates, a management consulting company. He was a visiting scholar at the Russell Sage

Foundation, visiting professor at Cornell University, and faculty member of the New School for Social Research. He lived in Los Angeles, California, and passed away in 2016. Mr. Toffler is quoted in Chapter 14.

Mary Waldon, MSW, LCSW

Mary Waldon is a Licensed Clinical Social Worker specializing in change-oriented psychotherapy and Dialectical Behavior Therapy for teenagers, young adults, and their families. She works extensively with mother/daughter relationships, helping women and their daughters strengthen communication and connection during the challenging teen years. Mary is a graduate of the University of Chicago's School of Social Service Administration and the clinical social work internship at Northwestern Memorial Hospital's Stone Institute of Psychiatry and the Outpatient Treatment Center. She sees patients privately and leads skills groups in Winnetka, Illinois. She is quoted in Chapter 8.

Dr. Stewart Wolf and John G. Bruhn

Interested in the mind-body connection, Dr. Wolf, a Professor and Chair of the Department of Medicine at the University of Oklahoma Health Sciences Center, and Mr. Bruhn, a Sociologist and Vice President for Academic Affairs at University of Texas, El Paso, studied a small Pennsylvania town of Italian immigrants called Roseto after they heard about its surprisingly low rate of heart disease. This "Roseto Effect" sites a happy, low-stress lifestyle, strong multigenerational family structures, and cohesive community life as sources for this phenomenon. He and Mr. Bruhn co-authored *The Power of Clan* and *The Roseto Story: An Anatomy of Health*. Throughout his career, Mr. Bruhn has published many studies and textbooks on topics about community and well-being. More information about their study can be found in Chapter 6.

BIBLIOGRAPHY

Adams, John. *Letters of John Adams to Abigail Adams*. 1780.

Barnard, Michael. *Secrets of the Sun – Millennial Meditations*. BoltPix Studios, 2013.

Burckhardt, Jacob. *The Civilization of the Renaissance in Italy*. 1860.

Churchill, Winston. *Speech: 'House of Commons Rebuilding'*. 1943.

Global Good News. *Maharishi's Holiday Message: 'Know thyself' through Transcendental Meditation*. 2004

Grossman, Ron and Charles Leroux. *A New `Roseto Effect'*. Chicago Tribune, 1996.

Institute of Vedic Architecture and City Planning. *Building for the Health and Happiness of Everyone*. Maharishi Vedic University, Ltd, 2001.

Institute of Vedic Architecture and City Planning. *Vastu Homes and Cities in Harmony with Natural Law*. Maharishi University of Management and Maharishi Vedic University Press, 2014.

Kurzweil, Ray. *The Singularity is Near*. Penguin, 2006.

Larry King Weekend. *Interview with Maharishi Mahesh Yogi*. CNN, 2002.

Lynch, David. *Catching the Big Fish: Meditation, Consciousness, and Creativity*. The Penguin Group, 2007.

Maharishi Mahesh Yogi. *Lecture: 'Building Fortune-Creating Homes and Workplaces: A Unified Field-Based Approach to Architecture'*. MERU, Holland, 2007.

Maharishi Mahesh Yogi. *Lecture: 'The growth of perception from multiplicity to duality to Unity, proceeding on the path from ignorance to enlightenment, the state of supreme knowledge'*. 1971.

Maharishi Mahesh Yogi. *Maharishi Speaks to Students – Mastery over Natural Law*. Maharishi Vedic University Press, 1997.

Maharishi Mahesh Yogi. *Science of Being and Art of Living*. Maharishi University of Management Press, 1963.

Nader, MD, PhD, Dr. Tony. *Human Physiology - Expression of Veda and the Vedic Literature*. Maharishi Vedic University, Ltd, 2000.

Oates, Robert. *Celebrating the Dawn*. Putnam, 1976.

Plowboy Interview. Mother Earth News, January/February 1986.

Seppa, Nathan. *The Mess That Is Stress*. Science News, 2015.

Thun-Honenstein, Christoph. Foreword of *Uneven Growth: Tactical Urbanisms for Expanding Megacities*. Pedro Gadanho, The Museum of Modern Art, New York, 2014.

Wolf, Stewart and Bruhn, John. *The Power of Clan: The Influence of Human Relationships on Heart Disease*. Transaction Publishers, 1998.

THANKS

My deepest thanks to those who have helped me reach the goal of writing this book.

Special thanks to Dr. Eike Hartmann, Wojtek Skalski, and Jonathan Lipman for their wonderful insights into Maharishi Vastu and their encouragement of this project.

To my Co-Editors, Michael W. Barnard and Lindsay Scherr Burgess, whose editorial skills and insights are remarkable.

To Julie Roth, for her help with copy editing.

To Angelo Pizzo, for his beautiful design aesthetic and wonderful patience throughout the process.

To Christian Schweizer, Alberto Castano, and Jonathon Phillips - your inspirational work is spreading an appreciation for Maharishi Vastu all over the world.

To Richard Bialosky, A.I.A., for his knowledge and dedication to Maharishi Vastu Development in Vero Beach, FL.

Thanks to Dr. John Hagelin, Dr. Neil Paterson, Dr. Bevin Morris, Dr. Bobby Roth, and Mr. David Lynch, all visionary leaders who have inspired the world to seek enlightenment.

To my brother S. Jacob Scherr, during his years of working at the Natural Resources Defense Council (NRDC), taught me and the world that the protection of the environment is our most important endeavor.

To Jonathan Burgess, whose visionary ideas about green development and architecture are inspiring a new generation of builders and developers.

To Stanley Black and Robert Barth, whose dedication to the community has set an example of enlightened philanthropy.

To Barbara Bartolozzi, the gifted Florentine tour guide, who brings the past to life through her extraordinary mind and heart. Her love and passion for the city of Florence, and her understanding of its history and art, have been a real gift to me on my journey of understanding the deeper origins of the Renaissance.

To my early readers Diana Broussard, Bayard Cartmell, Michael Mesnick, David Milner, Lincoln Norton, and Sally and Eric Rosenfeld, whose enthusiasm was greatly appreciated throughout this process.

To Adam Scherr and Marlyse Phlaum, who constantly surprise me with their inspired perspective on life and the promise of the next generation.

To Carole Dickert-Scherr, my sister-in-law, who has given so much love and created so much beauty that heaven on Earth seems plausible.

To Larry Delrose, a great friend and business associate whose advice is always wise and practical simultaneously.

To Tom and Debbie Gould, your encouragement on this project and the journey of life are indispensable.

To Mary Waldon, a special thanks, whose insight into human nature never ceases to amaze, and who brings clarity to the adventure of life.

To Heidi Krauss, who asked me a thousand times to write a book.

I thank all of you, who have generously given your time to read this book.

BEING TOGETHER

*I walked the streets of my memory. Roman streets
with people everywhere and giant cars, foreign
beasts battering ancient cobblestones.
I faintly remember what it was like to share
the streets and feel the energy of people
going through their day in a symphony
of togetherness. The fresh food and
flower markets bursting with abundant
flavors and smells. The piazza where one
could watch and feel the value of proportion,
symmetry, connection, and belief.
The sounds of chatter and playfulness.
Together, these Romans once conquered
the world by making the world part of them.*

*Today, our memory of being together is dormant,
overwhelmed by the busyness of our days, and the
need to rush through life – as if somehow that saves
time. The richness and intimacy we used to feel
with family and friends was once an interwoven
part of our daily adventure.*

*It is the drama of a community that helps each
individual experience the common thread that
binds us all together – the art and science of Being.*

*I dreamt that night of such a place, a Village that is
the expression outside of what we are inside.*

NOTES

59313463R00106

Made in the USA
Lexington, KY
31 December 2016